# The Called War

# Volume 1: Foundations

THE CALLED WAR

PROLOGUE BY

ADMIRE PROSPER MAKUYANA

BEANS ROBSON. T

Harare, Zimbabwe


THE CALLED WAR
Copyright©2020 Robson Tafara Beans

All scriptures are quoted from the King James and New American Standard Versions of the Holy Bible unless stated otherwise.

All rights reserved.

No part of this book may be reproduced or transmitted in any form by any means mechanical or electronic, including photocopying, duplicating, recording or by any information storage and retrieval system, without permission in writing from the publisher and copyright holders, except in the case of brief quotations embodied in critical articles or reviews.

ISBN: 9798648756229

# Acknowledgements

I would love to acknowledge the role of my parents in raising me to be the person I am today. I have learned a lot of things from my soft-spoken and exemplary father, Stephen Beans. The man sacrificed his whole life to make sure my siblings and I were comfortable growing up. I do not remember the number of times I was baptized by my father when I was young. Being an elder in the church, he would baptize people now and then so, I had a hobby. He carried me on the bicycle to these baptisms and every time I would get baptized. You are a role model.

My mother, Miracle Beans, did not tire in packing an additional set of clothes for the baptisms. I remember her reading from [Proverbs 13:24] before spanking me. Thank you for that. I will use the verse on your grandkids. One woman who has fought the devil on many fronts and has always come out on top. You are an inspiration.

Vimbai, Mavis, Tinashe, and Makanaka Beans, my siblings, I have learned a lot about relationships from you guys. I appreciate the fights now that I'm older. I love you guys.

I also want to acknowledge the guidance and mentorship I continue to receive from my father in the Lord, Apostle Steven Mandeya. It is a great blessing to learn from you, sir.

Special mention goes to the kings - Nokuthula Magwenzi, Trevor Mandeya, Mitchell Munyaradzi Gumbo, Prosper Makuyana, and Honest Zhanda. Nothing about this book made it to the print without their input. Let's walk on gents.

Brother Gaylord Terence Mazuruse, may you continue to be an inspiration to me and this generation. Your faithfulness and commitment are remarkable.

# Special Mentions

A lot of individuals and ministries have contributed to my spiritual growth and had a huge bearing on the writing of this book. Chief among them is Z.A.O.G.A F.I.F, the church I was born and raised in. I have seen a lot of miracles and deliverances through this ministry.

Faith Hill church, under the leadership of Pastors Tafara and Chipo Butayi, has also transformed me from extreme legalism into a balanced Christian. I continue to be inspired by the works of C.S Lewis, Pastor Vlad Savchuck, Ravi Zacharias, and Derek Prince.

# Dedication

I dedicate this book to all Christians that yearn for the unadulterated word of God, living in this post-modern relativistic world. Our faith has come under attack but, we stand for the FULL Gospel without compromise.

# Contents

# Prologue

I was born into an Anglican family and my church life was one I can describe as a normal one. My parents and I would go to church on Sundays and I would go to school during the week. I received secondary education at a Missionary school, where both my parents happened to teach. Essentially, my environment was largely the same. At a very young age, I developed a love for the Lord and I was very zealous. With the little knowledge about God that I had, I found myself being a founding member of a students' ministry - the Christian Union. Life was good; we would hold church services over the weekends and we would fast and pray during the week. Because it was a boarding school, we found ourselves knitting together a close group of brothers and sisters. We would spend most of our time together, and since some of us were from Pentecostal backgrounds, it began rubbing on all of us and we walked in the Pentecostal revelation. Speaking in tongues was normal and expected. Healing, prophecy, and sharing in the word was a part of everything we believed in.

Television was one source of inspiration in these early days. We would watch other ministers over the holidays and we began learning a lot. After High school, the Christian Union was ongoing but, under the leadership of some of the brothers that had joined along the way. I would visit from time to time and would share the word with the brothers. I was now living in the capital, Harare, and I had met other brethren with whom we were now holding intercession prayers. During one of these prayer sessions, a certain brother said something that surprised me. He said, "I'm going to lay hands on people and I sense some people are going to be delivered from demons." This came as a theological shock to me in many ways. In the twenty years of my church life, I had never really come across demons. The priests that had preached to me had never preached on demons and deliverance. Even up to now, I do not recall a single bible reading that had something to do with deliverance and demons. In our Christian Union, I believe some people that came from Pentecostal backgrounds had heard about demonology at some point but, I had not. This was a shock and it was interesting to me at the same time. I was saying to myself, "Well, I don't have a demon but let's see how this goes."

The brother went on to lay hands on another woman who was in the room and I had to pick my jaws off the floor. The lady started rolling on the floor and started saying things. It wasn't hard for me to understand that it wasn't the woman speaking but, the demon through the woman. This was the very first day I knew there were things like spiritual husbands that can lay a claim on someone. Given my background, this was an opening of another dimension in my life. It raised a lot of questions at the back of my mind and from then, it was something I wanted more information on.

After some time, we started a home prayer group that grew in numbers up to a point we decided to hold services on Sunday. A certain young lady visited us in one of our meetings and gave her life to Christ. It was a few days later that the lady's mother would ask me to pick up her daughter every time we had a prayer session. It was then that I learned that the young girl was a lesbian and was quite a problem at home. Being a young pastor, I was fascinated with the prospect of being backed up by the elderly. It meant we were doing something right. Every time we had prayer sessions  or Sunday services; I  would  pick  the  young lady up on my way.  Two weeks after her conversion, we  held  another Sunday service  but,  this  one  would change a lot of things in the lives of many people. The lady's life and mine included. It was one in which there was a strong presence of God. As we worshipped God, the  young  lady  started  shouting  and  rolling  on  the floor. She would roll on the floor and rise intermittently, saying strange things just like the first lady I had seen in the other prayer meeting. The only difference this time was that I was the leader and I had to take charge of the situation.

So, when I walked over to her, she leapt and grabbed my collar. About four male ushers ran to me to help me but, they could not even shake her off. From the other deliverance sessions, I had seen on television after I sought to understand more about demonology, I remembered something. I said, "In the name of Jesus, leave me." And, suddenly, she left me and began shouting saying "You are burning me." I remember some of the words clearly; she went on to mention that she was the queen of the ocean and that she was way older than all of us who were there. A lot of things were exposed; she was lesbian, rebellious and she was also failing in school. This was a deep revelation on demonology to me. We then went on to pray for her and it was one of the longest deliverance sessions I've been involved in. She would vomit and lie flat on the floor, then rise moments later under the influence of the demons. It took about an hour until she was fully delivered. Glory to God.

This experience gave me more information on how demons can affect the lives of their hosts but also raised another question. Why did it take so long for her to be delivered? Why did it take long? And how could demons be afflicting and affecting a believer? I went on for about one and a half years until I got a revelation on this subject. One night, after intercession, I went home and took a bath, preparing to sleep. It had been another normal day of prayer; nothing out of the ordinary and it had just been a normal prayer service. I said a very simple and short prayer in bed thanking the Lord for the day and then closed my eyes. What happened next is something I never really shared with people for the simple reason that I don't want to base my life solely on experiences. Yes, experiences are more real and have a deep personal impact but, they are not the whole map unless they are supported by the canon of scripture.

As soon as I closed my eyes, I had a night vision; darkness engulfed the room. It was not only literal darkness but, a heavy dark presence that I felt. I began suffocating, choking, and gasping for air. At that moment, I was thinking my end had come; I thought I was dying. Strangely, in this darkness, I could see a being I knew was the devil. He did not look like the picture we got from Sunday school or books. I didn't identify him because of the looks but, I just knew that I knew that I knew that it was the devil. What puzzled me in all this was why, as a Christian, I would die this way. Then I repeatedly shouted 'Jesus'. As I shouted this, there was a bright flash of light that broke into the darkness and a being I knew as Jesus appeared in the room. The suffocation eased but I was not free. It was just relief but I still felt I wasn't completely free. Jesus was in the room and I expected Him to deal with the devil but, to my surprise, He didn't do anything about the devil. I did not exchange words with Him about it but, I know I communicated this (it felt telepathic – for lack of a better word) and He handed me a rod. As soon as I received the rod, I just knew I had to use it and I did; I swung it aiming to strike the devil's head and mid-air, the rod turned into a sword that then struck him by the head. He fell then disappeared and I was completely free. The Lord just smiled and left. As I was trying to figure it all out, I got up and I was sweating profusely. It was in winter by I was drenched in sweat.

As any Bible-believing Christian, I wanted to check my experience against scripture. The Spirit led me to Mathew 28:18

*Then Jesus came to them and said, "All authority in heaven and on earth has been given to me. [19] Therefore go and make disciples of all nations, baptizing them in the name of the Father and of the Son and of the Holy Spirit, [20] and teaching them to obey everything I have commanded you. And surely I am with you always, to the very end of the age." NIV*

The great commission is a perfect explanation for delegated authority; the omnipotent God delegating ALL authority to our Lord Jesus and He, in turn, delegating that same authority to us. In this power, He instructs us to go and make disciples of all nations. His death and resurrection on the cross brought ALL power to His name, in which we operate. We are not waiting for power, we were given the power and we should exercise it against devils and demons. It is our responsibility to deal with demons, in Jesus' name. This was convincing but, I wanted more Scripture. I said, "Lord, I will not share this as your word if it's not confirmed by more scripture" and the Spirit again led me to Ephesians. Then He asked me, what your favourite scripture in this book and I said Ephesians 6:12. He then said this is where people are stuck because they take only the last part.

*Finally, be strong in the Lord and in the strength of His might. Put on the full armor of God, so that you will be able to stand firm against the schemes of the devil. For our struggle is not against flesh and blood, but against the rulers, against the powers, against the world forces of this darkness, against the spiritual forces of wickedness in the heavenly places. NASB*

The Spirit then made emphasis on verses 10 and 11; where it says, be strong in the Lord and in the power of His might. He began ministering to me that alone, we don't have any power; but we operate in delegated authority. He also emphasised the fact of putting on the whole armour of God. I didn't sleep that night until the early hours of the morning as I studied Scripture to fully grasp what He was saying to me. It was mind-blowing. From that day, as I preach, people are delivered from demons and even when I pray for the afflicted, it doesn't take time. It is this revelation of the delegated authority a believer has that has moved me into a life of victory over darkness

I remember one lady who had a relationship issue; Her long-time boyfriend has ended their relationship for no tangible reason and had completely cut ties and said no to any reconciliation. She came to me and asked for prayer. I wasn't going to pray for the boyfriend to come back; Human beings are free moral beings and can make their own choices but, if there was anything behind this, that's what we were going to pray against. So, I asked her to go on a week-long fast with me. This we did not to get power but, to bring ourselves closer to God to have more understanding of the situation. On the last day, she came for prayer and as I prayed, a demon manifested on her. Through her, the demon began speaking of its origins (the ocean once again) and how it had been controlling her family for a long time. There were also vows made against her including barrenness. She was then delivered and went home. In a week, the boyfriend called wanting her back. This was in June; In August, they engaged and in December that same year, they wedded. Hallelujah.

Scripture and experience in ministry has led me to understand that some believers give room to the devil in their lives mainly through

1.  Habitual sin

2.  Involvement in the occult.

I also want to say that the answer to whether or not a Christian can be afflicted/oppressed/demonized (not possessed) by demons can never be adequately answered by a simple Yes or No. Some terms need defining and some conditions need explaining. We can all be Christians but, some can be carnally minded and some spiritually-minded. Just like in Revelation, some can be cold, some hot and some lukewarm. The Called War explains this in more details, bringing the much-needed balance between theology and experience, guided by the canon of Scripture.

Pastor Admire Proper Makuyana

# Introduction

I was born and raised in a Christian family and I had a very good childhood. I started learning about many Christian doctrines as a child and I grew into it because of the influence of my parents but, I was not fully committed. In July 2009, on my way from a school sports trip, the bus we were in almost veered off the road and that marked the beginning of my conversion. I realised how quickly life can change and I promised myself to do something about it. I had received Christ in my early childhood but I felt it was not enough.

It was in August that same year that I attended a revival meeting hosted by Z.A.O.G.A Borrowdale in Harare that I gave my life to Christ, or rather, recommitted my life to Christ. That would take me on an exciting journey. I joined the Christian Union and later led it in my final high school year. A lot of young people served the Lord through this ministry. I then went on to be a co-leader in an interdenominational youth ministry together with my high school friends. This continued through college and at the same time, I got opportunities to preach in my family church.

From childhood to early adulthood, I had always believed spiritual warfare was all about going to the prayer mountain and spend the whole night binding devils or casting out demons. It was with this understanding that I ministered from Christian Union to College. It was after college that I started noticing patterns around my family and around people I was associated with. At one point I sat down with my father and asked about our family history and I was shocked to realise that he and some of his siblings had gone through the same things. All of them had been imprisoned at one point and in all cases, it was on false allegations. I consulted my brothers and father in the Lord who then started revealing some of the realities of cycles, strongholds and patterns that affect people.

It took me a while to process but from then, it was like a fire was ignited in me. I became so consumed with learning more about this and it led me to a lot of discoveries. Over time, I had prayed for demonized people and I had seen it happening and I thought that was all to Spiritual Warfare. I began realising that there was a more elaborate plan to it. It wasn't just praying in tongues at the top of our voices. I began realising the mistakes we make every day when we make decisions. I had also been exposed to teachings that claim that all is done when you receive the Lord Jesus as your personal Lord and Saviour. This, I found to be theologically correct but, it came into sharp disagreement with my experience.

As I said, my curiosity got even worse. I delved into the subject trying to harmonize my experience and what I had heard. In the end, my experiences don't define the Bible. The Bible explains my experiences and all my findings and the revelation I believe I got from the Lord culminated in this book. In the end, I realised that just like [Eph 6:12] states, we are in a continual state of war against an astute schemer who thrives on deception.

This book will take you from the origins to where you are today, in this very moment. How our forefathers have been fought, how you are being attacked in your nation, family and as an individual. Be patient as I build my case and I promise, you will also discover how to defend yourself and most importantly, how to attack.

Beans Robson. T

# Chapter One

The Cold War

This book borrows its name from a tense relationship between two major world powers (Russia and The United States) that lasted for nearly half a century, commonly known as the cold war. This is because the gist of this book is to explain a similar type of war that born again believers find themselves fighting in. I shall begin by briefly explaining what the cold war was as I build my case.

It must be noted that I do not claim to be a cold war authority and I would advise anyone seeking more information on the subject to consult other sources but, I will still just explain only the concept this book borrows.

As I mentioned earlier, there were two main antagonists in the cold war – The Soviet Union and The United States of America and one of the major reasons of this antagonism was over how people ought to be governed. The Soviet Union was led by communists and the Western capitalist democracies feared a spread of communism in Europe and eventually the whole world. In essence, it was a clash of ideologies.

It is not my aim to dwell on which form of government is best for humanity – for that needs a book on its own. And even after writing that book, one may still realise that it is a dilemma akin to having to choose between a red and a green apple – In the end, according to experts, they all taste slightly different and you just hope the one you pick does not have worms nesting in it. But, in passing, I will just mention the fact that the kingdom of God is not a democracy. What you do with that information is not my business.

So, one power believes in capitalism and the other believes in communism. I'm not sure if it would have been possible for both powers to just maintain their beliefs and not fight but, anyway, they did. The most interesting part is that the two main powers did not fight directly. They fought via what are called proxy wars.

*A proxy war is an armed conflict between two states or non-state actors which act on the instigation or on behalf of other parties that are not directly involved in the hostilities. In order for a conflict to be considered a proxy war, there must be a direct, long-term relationship between external actors and the belligerents involved. The aforementioned relationship usually takes the form of funding, military training, arms, or other forms of material assistance which assist a belligerent party in sustaining its war effort.*

A classic example of a proxy war that these two world giants fought in was the Vietnam war. The Vietnam War was ostensibly a civil war between the communist North and pro-Western South. Yet the Vietnamese didn't do all the fighting. The United States and many other countries intervened, propping up both sides—

but especially South Vietnam—with troops, weapons and supplies and turning what started as a small guerrilla uprising into a major Cold War-era conflict. The United States got involved to prevent South Vietnam from falling into communist hands. At first, the U.S. operated behind the scenes, but after 1964, sent combat troops and became more deeply mired in the war.

I have heard the words "Everyone loses in a war" and I do not know if this was the case in the cold war. All I know is that the world is predominantly capitalist and I have it on good authority that the Vietnamese suffered massive infrastructure losses and that lots of lives were lost in both camps. However, this is not the crux of this book. At this point, I have explained the concept that I borrow from this historic clash.

1. A cold war: We have established that it is an indirect hostility between parties(nations, individuals or groups of people)
2. Proxy wars: Direct clashes between parties, each sponsored or supported by external powers or forces.

War

All along I have been writing under the assumption that the reader has a rudimentary appreciation of what war is. But, I do not see any harm done by just shedding more light on some specifics about war as I continue to build on my case. The root of the English word 'war', *werra*, is Frankish-German, meaning confusion, discord, or strife, and the verb *werran* meaning to confuse or perplex. War certainly generates confusion, as Clausewitz noted calling it the "fog of war", but that does not discredit the notion that war is organized, to begin with.

War is characterised by battles – armed combat between parties. Thus war is generally characterised by several or multiple battles. Battles generally are well defined in duration, area, and force commitment. Wars and military campaigns are guided by strategy, whereas battles take place on a level of planning and execution known as operational mobility. German strategist Carl von Clausewitz stated that "the employment of battles ... to achieve the object of war was the essence of strategy".

Strategy
Every war has a mission/goal, a reason for fighting and the attainment of the goal is decided by a lot of factors. Chief among the factors is strategy. There is a discipline now in some defence colleges called Military Science which focuses on many aspects of war including strategy. This just goes to show how important strategy is when it comes to war. How good a strategy is and how well the strategy is executed are huge factors in determining how the war ends.

So what also implicitly becomes important are the players. From the strategists to the walking soldiers. Military technology, resources supply, quality of training etc. all become decisive factors in war. There is one statement by Sun Tzu, a Chinese general, military strategist, writer and philosopher who lived in the Eastern Zhou period of ancient China that I would want to quote at this stage:

*"All warfare is based on deception. Hence, when we are able to attack, we must seem unable; when using our forces, we must appear inactive; when we are near, we must make the enemy believe we are far away; when far away, we must make him believe we are near."*

# Chapter Two

## The Called War

The born again Christian finds himself a new creature [2 Cor 5:17], bought with a special price [1 Cor 6:20] and with a ticket to heaven [Heb 11:6] in the after-life but strangely, at war in this life [Eph 6:12]. One would imagine that at some point in the Christian walk there is a cease-fire or some peace treaty signed but, not at all. This is a war that is fought to the death and it is not only for new believers but even the seasoned.

Tongues, no doubt will arm you better, but you will still be in the trenches and no one chooses. It is inherent. The day you accept the Lord Jesus as your personal Lord and saviour is the day you are enrolled in the Army-Navy, Seals or Marines you pick what you want. The other party does not care.

The Bible speaks of a party in heaven when a new soul comes to Christ [Luke 15:10] and the love a new believer receives (especially in a church setting) is indeed the best thing fellow Christians can do. But, it is almost an anti-climax a few steps in the Christian walk when the baby Christian finds themselves at the receiving end of a barrage of enemy fire. Only if they listen to sermons or read Scripture on their own they will find the greatest(in my opinion) writer of the New Testament(in which they live) mentioning something different from the celebrations of regeneration. The Apostle Paul in [*2 Cor. 10:3-5*] puts it succinctly:

*"For though we live in the world, we do not wage war as the world does. The weapons we fight with are not the weapons of the world. On the contrary, they have divine power to demolish strongholds. We demolish arguments and every pretension that sets itself up against the knowledge of God, and we take captive every thought to make it obedient to Christ."*

It is almost as if Paul just mentions this in passing. There are several facts that he states in this passage of scripture.

1.  We live in the world.
2.  We are in a state of war
3.  We have weapons (which are powerful)
4.  We war against arguments
5.  We fight to bring these arguments into the obedience of Christ

It's quite a sobering realisation. And if you are one not to build a doctrine from a single verse in the Bible, here is one more verse that will clear the doubt

*"Put on the full armor of God, so that you can take your stand against the devil's schemes. For our struggle is not against flesh and blood, but against the rulers, against the authorities, against the powers of this dark world and against the spiritual forces of evil in the heavenly realms. Therefore put on the full armour of God, so that when the day of evil comes, you may be*

*able to stand your ground, and after you have done everything, to stand. Stand firm then, with the belt of truth buckled around your waist, with the breastplate of righteousness in place, and with your feet fitted with the readiness that comes from the gospel of peace. In addition to all this, take up the shield of faith, with which you can extinguish all the flaming arrows of the evil one. Take the helmet of salvation and the sword of the Spirit, which is the word of God."*

In his letter to the Ephesians, the Apostle reiterates some of the facts he mentioned to the church at Corinth and he also sheds light on the reality that we are at war.

1. We have armour. And we have to put it on. It's of no use to have the shining armour and not wear it.
2. We are being and we will be attacked by the devil.
3. The devil uses schemes to attack
4. Again, we are not fighting against people, but evil authorities, powers.
5. He details the armour that we have for both defence and offence.

Paul mentions the same facts in some of his letters, like the first one he wrote to Timothy. But, let us hear it from other New Testament writers.

*"Be self-controlled and alert. Your enemy the devil prowls around like a roaring lion looking for someone*

*to devour. Resist him, standing firm in the faith." [1 Pet. 5:8-9]*

*"Submit yourselves to God. Resist the devil, and he will flee from you." [James 4:7]*

Apostles Peter and James know this too. It's not Paul's nature of writing after all. The apostle Peter in 1 Pet. 5:8 reminds of a common scene in almost all war movies where soldiers take turns to be on watch duty. You can almost tell what will happen next when you see the soldier on watch drinking alcohol or falling asleep – death.

So Apostle Peter instructs the Christian to be alert and to be sober and what he states without verbalising it is that we are in a state of war.

Alright, we are in a state of war. Fair enough, the new believer perhaps didn't read the fine print. But, the puzzling thing is why? So at this point, the new believer acknowledges the fact that he is in a state of war. He also knows he has the armour and he knows what he is fighting against – arguments and the devil. But it is not so clear. Is it two different enemies? And another puzzle for him to solve is why is he fighting this war.

It is easy to come to the not so accurate conclusions. One might conclude that it is because their conversion was considered as rebellion or treason and is being punished. Another may simply think it is because good has to fight evil. But why does the war never end? Because more than two thousand years later after the cross, people are still fighting in it. If every other Christian is fighting in the war, where is the battlefield? What is our strategy? Who is leading us?

Let us go back to where it started.

# Chapter Three

Back to Creation

Man has always struggled with basically four questions – Origin, Purpose, Morality and Destiny. Whether you are educated or not, male or female, poor or rich, slave or free, black or any race. Man has a deep yearning to know where he came from, why he is here, how he should conduct himself and ultimately what the end game is.

There are several beliefs as to how the Universe came into existence and it is not the aim of this book to focus on that. I am a Christian writer and I believe in the Bible as the ultimate authority and I believe in God, the creator of everything there is.

So from the book of Genesis, we gather that God created the heavens and the earth. He then went on to create man in His image. [Genesis 1:27]. But before all this, there are some theological theories I would like to explain. I have to state that I do not think it matters which theory you believe in the most. In the grand scheme of things (salvation and eternal life), they do not matter and also, for this book, it doesn't matter much.

The theories arise from a problem created by science and the Bible. Scientists claim that the earth has been around for billions of years while the Biblical narrative points to a young earth, created only thousands of years back. To reconcile this gap, theories (and revelations) have been put forward and theologically, each has had its support and criticisms as well. I have one I believe makes sense and I will make a case for it. I must mention, at this point, that I will believe the Bible more than science any day. Revelation, by nature, is progressive so, I am willing to learn more about this subject even now and in the future. But, here it goes:

The Gap theory
Specifics may vary from source to source but the core fundamentals for the gap theory are:

1. There is a gap of possibly millions of years between Genesis 1:1 and Genesis 1:2
2. There is a pre-Adamic race that lived on the earth between Genesis 1:1 and Genesis 1:2.

The Apologetics press puts it this way:

The widely held view among gap theorists today is that the original creation of the world by God, as recorded in Genesis 1:1, took place billions of years ago. The creation was despoiled because of Satan's rebellion against God, resulting in his being cast from heaven with his followers. A cataclysm occurred at the time of Satan's overthrow and is said to have left the Earth in darkness (the "waste and void" of Genesis 1:2). [NOTE: It is alleged by some Gap theorists that the cataclysm occurring at Satan's overthrow terminated the geologic ages, after which God "re-created." It is alleged by others that the cataclysm occurred first, and then was followed by the geologic ages, after which God "re-created."] The world as God had created it, with all its inhabitants, was destroyed, which, it is claimed, accounts for the myriad fossils present in the Earth. Many holding to this theory place the fossils of dinosaurs, so-called "ape-men," and other extinct forms of life in this gap. Then, God "re-created" the Earth in six literal days. By way of summary, then, the "gap" between Genesis 1:1 and Genesis 1:2 contains the story of an original creation, a judgment, and ruination, while the verses in Genesis 1:3 through the remainder of the chapter record the story of the Earth's re-creation.

*Arguments Presented in Support of the Gap Theory*
Advocates of the Gap Theory base their beliefs on several arguments, a summary of which is given here; comments and refutation follow.

1. Gap theorists suggest that the word *bara* (used in Genesis 1:1, 21, 27) must mean "to create" (i.e.: *ex nihilo* creation), while the word *asah* cannot mean "to create," but rather means "to make." Therefore, the original creation was "created"; the creation of the six days was "made" (i.e., "made over").

2. Gap theorists suggest that the Hebrew verb *hayetha* (translated "was" in Genesis 1:2) should be rendered "became" or "had become"—a translation required to suggest a change of state from the original perfect creation to the chaotic conditions implied in verse 2.

3.  Gap theorists believe that the "without form and void" of Genesis 1:2 (*tohu wabohu*) can refer only to something once in a state of repair, but now ruined. Pember accepted these words as expressing "an outpouring of the wrath of God." Gap theorists believe that the cataclysm that occurred was on the Earth, and was the direct result of Satan's rebellion against God. The cataclysm, of course, is essential to the Gap Theory. Isaiah 14:12-15 and Ezekiel 28:11-17 are used as proof-texts to bolster the theory.

4.  Gap theorists believe that Isaiah 45:18 ("God created the earth not in vain"—tohu; the same word translated "without form" in Genesis 1:2) indicates that the Earth was not tohu at the initial creation. Therefore, they suggest, Genesis 1:2 can refer only to a judgment brought upon the Earth by God.

5.  Gap theorists generally believe that there was a pre-Adamic creation of both non-human and human forms—a position adopted to account for the fossils present in the geologic strata.

### The Day-Age theory

According to several sources, this theory holds that the six days referred to in the Genesis account of creation are not ordinary 24 hour days, but are much longer periods (of thousands or millions of years). In this way, the Genesis account is reconciled with the scientifically accepted age of the earth. The arguments for this theory revolve around the meaning of the Hebrew word "yom". Proponents of this theory point out that "yom" can have several meanings: twenty-four hour period, long age, etc. They often cite Psalm 90:4 and II Peter 3:8. To apply these verses as evidence would be out of context however, as both verses are using a simile to show that God is not constrained by the same time parameters as humans are. Back to "Yom", here is the breakdown:

1. "Yom" occurs 2,282 times outside of Genesis 1. It occurs 359 times with a number outside Genesis 1. In all 359 cases, the context clearly shows that a 24 hour day is being referenced.
3. "Yom" occurs 19 times outside of Genesis 1, together with the word "morning" or "evening". In all 19 cases, a 24 hour day is clearly intended. The words "morning" and "evening" occur together, without "day" 38 times outside of Genesis 1. Each of these occurrences refers to a 24 hour day.

"Yom" occurs with the word "night" 53 times outside of Genesis  Each of these occurrences refers to a 24 hour day.

I love this quote from an article in *Creation Day* regarding this issue: "Given this immense contextual evidence, one is tempted to ask somewhat flippantly, 'What could God have done to emphasize that the days of Genesis 1 are literal 24 hour days?' Might I suggest that He could have used the Hebrew "Yom" together with numbers, morning, evening or night? And that is exactly what He did!"

The Young Earth Theory

Young Earth creationism (YEC) is a form of creationism which holds as a central tenet that the Earth and its life forms were created in their present forms by God between approximately 6,000 and 10,000 years ago. In its most widespread version, YEC is based on the religious belief in the inerrancy of certain literal interpretations of the Book of Genesis. Its primary adherents are Christians who believe that God created the Earth in six days, in contrast with old-Earth creationism (OEC), which holds literal interpretations of Genesis that are compatible with the scientifically determined ages of the Earth and universe.

Now that we have talked about the main three theories, I must state that from where I stand right now, the Gap theory makes sense for me and I am one of its proponents. Let us then go straight into familiar territory – somewhere all Christians meet and agree on. As I said, the foundation of this book is not on any of the aforementioned theories but on the scriptural spiritual warfare we, as Christians, find ourselves in.

So if you are a gap theorist, after Genesis 1:1, come verse 2 and there is no debate from verse two. If you believe in the Day-Age theory, there is no debate about whether God created nature from verse two but only an argument over the length of the days. To me, that is not an issue because, whether or not it was 24 hours or any period, the bottom line is that God did create. And if you are a YEC proponent, there is no debate at all.

The Creation of Man
So, finally, we start with all nature created. Then in verse 27, man is created.

[Gen 1:26-28 KJV] *26 And God said, Let us make man in <u>our image, after our likeness</u>: and let them have dominion over the fish of the sea, and over the fowl of the air, and over the cattle, and over all the earth, and over every creeping thing that creepeth upon the earth. 27 So God created man <u>in his [own] image, in the image of God created he him; male and female created he them</u>. 28 And God blessed them, and God said unto them, Be fruitful, and multiply, and replenish the earth, and subdue it: and have dominion over the fish of the sea, and over the fowl of the air, and over every living thing that moveth upon the earth.*

Now God created man in His image and likeness. There are a few things to note here. There has been confusion to some people about Genesis 1:27 and Genesis 2:7

*And the LORD God formed man of the dust of the ground, and breathed into his nostrils the breath of life; and man became a living soul.*

The major question posed about these two is if they are two different accounts of the creation of man. The confusion is compounded by the difference in the order in which nature is created in Genesis 1 and in Genesis. This appears to be a contradiction in the translations that we read today because of the problem with translating – losing some important information. Some people would argue over [Genesis 2:19]

*Out of the ground the Lord God formed every beast of the field and every bird of the air, and brought them to Adam to see what he would call them.*

They usually say that this means God, in Chapter 2, is said to have created the animals after man, which contradicts the account of creation in Chapter 1. However, it is to be noted that the original Hebrew word used for form is the word *yatsar.* This word can be translated both in its perfect and pluperfect forms and is translated in the latter, would read:

*Out of the ground the Lord God had formed every beast of the field and every bird of the air, and brought them to Adam to see what he would call them.*

So, reconciling Genesis 1:27 and Genesis 2:7, we get to understand that the former gives a summary of the creation of man while the latter gives a detailed account of man's creation.

Now that we have settled this, the next big thing will be understanding what it means to be created in the image of God. I promise you this is a popular topic among Christians and Theologians as well. Some doctrines have taught that the image of God is physical. This is not the case. God is Spirit. [John 4:24],

Some scholars and doctrines have written in defence of this view basing on the Hebrew word for image, *tselem*, which was used in some parts of the Bible (Old Testament) to refer to idols or models. But, again [Ex. 20:1-4] and [Deut. 4:15-16] go on further to solidify the fact that the image of God(*imago Dei* in Latin) refers to a nonphysical component of man. More verses support this. [Luke 24:39; cf. Matthew 16:17]

Let me say that the *imago Dei* is one of the great mysteries of being human. We may only be able to understand this mystery in part. However, I will go ahead and mention part of what the image of God is.

1. Speech: One of the greatest miracles of humanity is the ability to speak. No animal speaks like humans and unfortunately, because we have been speaking for a long time we take it for granted that it is a miracle on its own. This enables us to manipulate language and communicate on a much deeper level. Animals may communicate but no animal can use language creatively to express emotions and feelings in the way of poems and music. No animal can give instructions or converse at the same depth as humans. God in the Bible spoke on many occasions. The whole account of creation was brought forth by His words. He spoke things into existence. Further reading: [Luke 24:39],[Matthew 16:17]

2. Creativity: The whole account of creation is about creativity. God creating the universe from

nothing. The earth and all its splendour. The magnificence of the stars. The perfect balance of the universe. The beauty of Homeostasis. And man is creative too, though on a different level. Beethoven's symphony, Mozart, Picasso, the great pyramids of Egypt, aeroplanes, rockets, computers e.t.c. No other animal can be as creative as a man. Animals only act on instinct.

3. Intelligence: In this regard, the difference is not that other animals cannot think, but that none of them can think like the human being. A biologist by the name John N. Moore put it in this way:

*The purest and most complex manifestation of man's symbolic nature is his capacity for conceptual thought, that is, for thought involving sustained and high order abstraction and generalization. Conceptual thought enables man to make himself independent of stimulus boundness that characterizes animal thinking. Animals, especially primates, give undeniable evidence of something analogous to human thought—analogous yet medically different in that their thought is bound to the immediate stimulus situation and to the felt impulse of the organism. Animal thinking, too, is riveted to the realm of survival (broadly taken) and therefore encompasses a variety of needs pertinent to the species as well as to the individual. These differences account for the distinction between conceptual thought, which is the exclusive prerogative of man, and perceptual thought, a cognitive function based directly upon sense perception, which man shares with animals (p. 344, emp. in orig.).*

Have you ever wondered why animals cannot be righteous or sinful? It is down to the fact that animals can never, at an intellectual level, perceive that there is a creator behind the world and everything therein.

*"Do not be like the horse and mule which have no understanding but must be controlled by bit and bridle"* [Ps 32:8-9]

4. Free Moral Agency: We are sentient being that is self-conscious and can make personal decisions. We are not hardwired primates. This is also called free will. It gives us the ability to chart our course and decide our destiny. This is highlighted by the apostle Paul in his letter to Timothy

   "who wants all people to be saved and to come to know the truth fully." [1 Timothy 2:4]

   God is has given us the choice to not choose Him. Let me just give a note: Sometimes free will is our greatest judgement, if not used in Wisdom.

5. Morality: Every man on earth has been haunted by the sense of right and wrong, justice and fairness. In our daily living, there is an uncomfortable reality that we face. That we

ought to behave in a certain way but we find ourselves, more often, behaving differently. On top of that, we tend to try and explain the causes of bad behaviour and not good behaviour.

We are made in the image of God, who is Himself perfect [Matthew 5:48], unchanging and good [Psalm 90:2], [1 Timothy 1:17] and unchanging.

6. Conscience: In the book of Romans Chapter 2, the Apostle Paul mentioned something very peculiar in verse 14. The New International Version says:

*"Indeed when the Gentiles who do not have the law do by nature things required by the law they are a lot for themselves even though they do not have the law they show that the requirements of the law are written on Their Hearts they are consciences also bearing witness and their thoughts sometimes."*

This passage points to the fact that even without a set of rules, man feels in him that there is a right code of conduct and a bad one. On top of that, man has a conscience something that tells him if what he's done is right or what he's done is wrong. He has feelings of guilt when he violates his conscience.

Conscience judges our actions whether they agree with our moral standards [1 Sam 24:5], [2 Sam. 24:10]. It executes that judgment within a person's soul as guilt, shame and estrangement from God [Psa. 32:4]. We can find some valuable information from a book by Guy N. Woods' book, Questions and Answers.

*Conscience is thus a safe guide in ascertaining whether our conduct is in harmony with our judgement; and, so long as it is not allowed to become hardened, seared over and callous, it serves effectively in the area which God designed for it. But, it was not intended to serve as a standard of right and wrong; and, it is not a "creature of education" so as to be equipped for such action. If we think what we are doing is right, we have a good conscience [Acts 23:1], [I Tim. 1:5,19], [Heb. 13:18],[I Pet. 3:16,21], a pure conscience [I Tim. 3:9], [II Tim. 1:3] and a conscience void of offence [Acts 24:16]. If we think we are doing wrong, our conscience is evil [I Tim. 4:2]. What we think, however, does not determine what is right and wrong and, like Paul when he persecuted the saints, we may have "a good conscience" although we are grievously in error. In such instances, it is the judgement which is at fault, and which must be "educated." When this is done, the conscience will swing around and approve that which it formerly condemned, and oppose that which it before approved.... It is wrong to disregard the promptings of our conscience, because it is designed to lead us to review our judgement; but, it is our judgement (our concept of right and wrong) which determines whether the conscience approves or condemns us (1976, pp. 213-214, emp. in orig.)*

7. An inclination to worship. Man has an innate desire to worship something. In different civilisations, man has always worshipped something. The object of worship is the only thing that differs from society to society but, the bottom line is that man is hard-wired to worship something. Some have even gone to the extent of worshipping themselves. Another pointer to this is the general gradation of things. The fact that there seem to be grades for everything in nature e.g. temperature is read on a scale. This points to the fact that there is a higher power above humans. In their text, Infidels and Heretics: An Agnostic's Anthology, Clarence Darrow and Wallace Rice quoted the famous sceptic, John Tyndall:

*Religion lives not by the force and aid of dogma, but because it is ingrained in the nature of man. To draw a metaphor from metallurgy, the moulds have been broken and reconstructed over and over again, but the molten ore abides in the ladle of humanity. An influence so deep and permanent is not likely soon to disappear... (1929, p. 146, emp. added).*

Now that we have talked about the imago Dei, we still haven't answered the other questions raised from the very first chapter. Trust me; it will all be clear after we rightly divide the word of truth from the foundations.

So when man was created, in [Genesis 1:27], the first thing that God told man was this:

*God blessed them and said to them, "Be fruitful and increase in number; fill the earth and subdue it. Rule over the fish in the sea and the birds in the sky and over every living creature that moves on the ground."*

Man was given a duty to be fruitful – to be productive. To multiply and fill the whole earth and to be the ruler of nature. It has to be noted that his dominion is not the imago Dei, but he was qualified to dominate the earth because of the imago Dei in which he was already created. He was also then given food for subsistence.

*" Then God said, "Behold, I have given you every plant yielding seed that is on the surface of all the earth, and every tree [which has fruit yielding seed; it shall be food for you; and to every beast of the earth and to every bird of the sky and to everything that moves on the earth which has life, I have given every green plant for food"; and it was so. God saw all that He had made, and behold, it was very good. And there was evening and there was morning, the sixth day.*

There is another responsibility given to man in this portion of Scripture. Man was tasked with ensuring that there was enough food for him and the animals. To him was given seed-bearing plants for food. It does not mean animals do not have to eat anything with seed in it but it means that in as much as animals can eat, I believe that man has the responsibility to plant from the seed after eating – to ensure there is always enough to eat. Going to [Genesis 2:7], a command concerning food is given:

*The Lord God commanded the man, saying, "From any tree of the garden you may eat freely; [17] but from the tree of the knowledge of good and evil you shall not eat, for in the day that you eat from it you will surely die."*

So, man is given an order. He could eat of any fruit in the garden but one. It is quite interesting to note that the first man seems to have been given a plant-based diet. I'm not in any way saying you must be a vegetarian or a vegan. I am simply observing what Scripture says. And I am definitely not trying to make a doctrine out of this. It is just an observation for those that love knowledge. The total number of trees in the garden of Eden was not mentioned. No-one knows how many were they and what type were they but, two special trees are mentioned that are significant in man's development.

The first one is the tree of life and the other one is the tree of the knowledge of good and evil. [Genesis 2:9].

A question may be made. Why would God create a tree that He did not want them to eat? Furthermore, why would God put it right in their faces?

To answer these questions, we must establish why man was created.

The fact that there is a purpose for anything automatically creates a concept of abuse. If I set out to go to a certain place, for instance, the local barber, it follows that any route I take that does not lead to the barber, in my case, a wrong route. It also follows that if God had a purpose in creating man, then there are other things man could do that were not part of His purpose.

I am a strong Liverpool supporter and at Anfield, the club's stadium, there are statues of past managers who were successful. There is a statue of Bill Shankly and that of Bob Paisley. They were successful to the point that they etched their names in the annals of the club's history and their legacy is still talked about today. Everyone who visits Anfield on any day is reminded of these men by their statues. When God made man in His image, He wanted him to represent Him on earth. God wanted man to be His vice-regent on earth. In other words, God wanted man to do, on a finite level, what He does on an infinite level. It has to be noted that an image is not in itself the object that it resembles.

Because He is autonomous and is indeed free of any influence, man also, in His image is a free moral agent and by that, he had to choose whether or not he wanted to be God's vice-regent.

Just as the Lord said to the nation of Israel in [Duet 30:19]:

"I call heaven and earth as witnesses today against you, that I have set before you life and death, blessing and cursing; therefore choose life, that both you and your descendants may live;"

The Lord also set death and life in the eyes of Adam and Eve. There is one thing about free will that will be clearly understood in the words of C.S Lewis:

"God created things which had free will. That means creatures which can go wrong or right. Some people think they can imagine a creature which was free but had no possibility of going wrong, but I can't. If a thing is free to be good it's also free to be bad. And free will is what has made evil possible. Why, then, did God give them free will? Because free will, though it makes evil possible, is also the only thing that makes possible any love or goodness or joy worth having. A world of automata -of creatures that worked like machines- would hardly be worth creating. The happiness which God designs for His higher creatures is the happiness of being freely, voluntarily united to Him and to each other in an ecstasy of love and delight compared with which the most rapturous love between a man and a woman on this earth is mere milk and water. And for that, they've got to be free. Of course, God knew what would happen if they used their freedom the wrong way: apparently, He thought it worth the risk. (...) If God thinks this state of war in the universe a price worth paying for free will -that is, for making a real world in which creatures can do real good or harm and something of real importance can *happen, instead of a toy world which only moves when He pulls the strings- then we may take it it is worth paying."*

So, man was created with the ability not to choose what God wanted. He instructs them to eat of any other tree they wanted except the tree of the knowledge of good and evil. So, some of the things we understand from man's way of living before the fall in the garden are these:

1.  Man did not know good and evil.
2.  Man only acted on God's instruction. Man did what God instructed Him to do. In a way, we can conclude man was dependant on God and lived his purpose.

But, even with man living his purpose, God still, in His permissive Will, allowed it for man to choose his own will. By choosing his own will man would essentially be choosing independence from God. And independence from God is death because God Himself is the giver and source of life. God cannot give anyone any life outside of Him for the simple reason that it doesn't exist.

This is why the Apostle Paul in [Romans 8:4] says

*For all who are being led by the Spirit of God, these are sons of God. NASB*

From the beginning, God had intended man to live from His guidance and it is the case when we are born again. Let us keep on building on this. Hallelujah.

# Chapter Four

The fall of Man.


*[Genesis 3:1-7] Now <u>the serpent was more crafty</u> than any beast of the field which the Lord <u>God had made</u>. And he said to the woman, "Indeed, has God said, 'You shall not eat from any tree of the garden'?"² The woman said to the serpent, "From the fruit of the trees of the garden we may eat;³ but from the fruit of the tree which is in the middle of the garden, God has said, 'You shall not eat from it or touch it, or you will die.'"⁴ The serpent said to the woman, "<u>You surely will not die!⁵ For God <u>knows that in the day you eat from it your eyes will be opened, and you will be like God, knowing good and evil.</u>"⁶ When the woman saw that the tree was good for food, and that it was a delight to the eyes, and that the tree was desirable to make one wise, she took from its fruit and ate; and she gave also to her husband with her, and he ate.⁷ Then the eyes of both of them were opened, and they knew that they were naked; and they sewed fig leaves together and made themselves loin coverings. NASB*

This is where it all started. And this is where the whole warfare started. From creation to this point, everything created was good. In fact, everything was very good. Then we realise there was a more crafty beast that God had made who knew something that these two people did not know. This beast also accuses God of hiding information from Adam and Eve. This serpent also appears to have been in a similar situation. The serpent says "You surely will not die!" This statement suggests the serpent either has been there before and he claims to have found that the death threat was propaganda. This is how the serpent presents his case.

So, if you were following clearly, there is an obvious question. Where did this being come from? From where does it know this? As far as we know, at this point, all animals were named by Adam himself.

Does this portion of scripture refer to the serpent as we know it? Now, there is a Scripture in the book of [Revelation 12:9-10] that describes Satan as the serpent.

*And the great dragon was thrown down, the serpent of old who is called the devil and Satan, who deceives the whole world; he was thrown down to the earth, and his angels were thrown down with him. [10] Then I heard a loud voice in heaven, saying,*

*"Now the salvation, and the power, and the kingdom of our God and the authority of His Christ have come, for the accuser of our brethren has been thrown down, he who accuses them before our God day and night.NASB.*

But, let us consult more Scripture on this subject. We know of a physical animal and Rev 12:9 is talking of Satan, another entity. So are they the same or two different creatures? Satan is not a physical being, although he can operate in the physical realm [Job 1-2]. He is a spiritual being that operates in the spiritual realm as evidenced in many passages that detail his spiritual attributes, such as [1 Peter 5:8], [Matthew 16:23], [ Acts 5:3] and [Ephesians 6:12].

*[Luke 22:3] And Satan entered into Judas who was called Iscariot, belonging to the number of the twelve. (NASB)*

[Matthew 16:23] *But He turned and said to Peter, "Get behind Me, Satan! You are a stumbling block to Me; for you are not setting your mind on God's interests, but man's."*

From a careful study of these passages, there is a concept that we learn. A concept that Pentecostals will call possession. Satan can enter into and influence physical beings. Spirits can indeed influence physical beings. [Numbers 22:28]

Let us look at one more passage. [Ezekiel 28] narrates the words spoken by God by the prophet Ezekiel concerning Tyre and Sidon. From verse 1 to 10, the word of the Lord concerns the leader of Tyre. Then from verse 11 to 19, the word of the Lord is directed to the King of Tyre.

*Again the word of the Lord came to me saying, [12] "Son of man, take up a lamentation over the king of Tyre and say to him, 'Thus says the Lord God,*

*"You had the seal of perfection, Full of wisdom and perfect                         in                         beauty. [13] "You were in Eden, the garden of God; every precious stone was your covering: the ruby, the topaz and the*

diamond;
The beryl, the onyx and the jasper; the lapis lazuli, the turquoise and the emerald; and the gold, the workmanship of your settings and sockets, was in you. On the day that you were created they were prepared.
14 "You were the anointed cherub who covers, and I placed you there. You were on the holy mountain of God; you walked in the midst of the stones of fire.
15 "You were blameless in your ways from the day you were created until unrighteousness was found in you.
16 "By the abundance of your trade you were internally filled with violence, and you sinned; therefore I have cast you as profane from the mountain of God. And I have destroyed you, O covering cherub, from the midst of the stones of fire.
17 "Your heart was lifted up because of your beauty; You corrupted your wisdom by reason of your splendor.
I cast you to the ground; I put you before kings, that they may see you.
18 "By the multitude of your iniquities, in the unrighteousness of your trade. You profaned your sanctuaries.
Therefore I have brought fire from the midst of you; It has consumed you, And I have turned you to ashes on the earth
In the eyes of all who see you. 19 "All who know you among the peoples are appalled at you; you have become terrified
and you will cease to be forever."'"

This chapter reveals to us something interesting. God says, in verse 13, that the King of Tyre was once in Eden. But the king of Tyre was never in Eden. It was Adam, Eve and the serpent. He also says(verse 120, he had the seal of perfection – which he never had. The King of Tyre was never a perfect model. So, in essence, God was referring to a king behind the king of Tyre. God was addressing the spirit influencing the King of Tyre, just like the Lord Jesus confronted Satan who was influencing Peter [Matt 16:23].

A similar address is found in the book of Isaiah in the 14th chapter when God was addressing the King of Babylon.

Martin Luther states it this way:

*Let us, therefore, establish in the first place that the serpent is a real serpent, but one that has been entered and taken over by Satan.*

*The Bible tells us that Satan used a real serpent to deceive Eve. And because of his entrance into the serpent, he can rightly be called the "serpent of old" or "great dragon" in Revelation.*

Just as a side note, this is where the Gap Theory that we talked about in the previous chapters harmonises the pre-Adamic race and the fall of man. In the Gap Theory, Satan is sent to the pre-Adamic race for reasons similar to why Jesus was sent to the world. It is believed that instead of representing God here on earth, he rebelled against God together with the whole race and they worshipped him instead of God. This led to the Lord destroying the whole race in a flood, whose residue we find in Genesis 1 verse 2.

Remember we said this is not the thrust of this book. I just mentioned it for the sake of those that want to make sense of many things like me.

Now that we have established where Satan came into the picture, let us conclude why he claimed to have been in a similar situation to Adam and Eve.

Let us draw a parallel between him and the first man.

- They were both created perfect and started out living their purposes. [Gen 1:31], [Eze 28:12-13]

The devil then fell from grace. [Isaiah 14:12-14]

*"How you have fallen from heaven, O star of the morning, son of the dawn! You have been cut down to the earth, You who have weakened the nations![13] "But you said in your heart, 'I will ascend to heaven; I will raise my throne above the stars of God, And I will sit on the mount of assembly In the recesses of the north. [14] 'I will ascend above the heights of the clouds; I will make myself like the Most High.'"*

Satan fell because he tried to make himself like God. That was his downfall. And he shows up in the garden of Eden with the same trap. Ladies and gentlemen, the only thing Satan did not say was that he was an example of the rebellion he was seducing them into.

How often do we hear our friends and co-workers saying, "I did it and I'm here?" I have heard that a lot. Or they say "It's not like people say it is." In my experience, these statements are made when someone is being seduced into something addictive like cocaine. The only thing the enablers talk about is the high you get and they never talk about the possible addiction that can easily follow.

This is the same thing Satan does. And it is amazing to see how innocence yields to a suggestion without even putting up a fight. Growing up, there were a lot of things we were told by our parents in my Shona culture. They used to tell us not to sit or play on the roads and when we asked why they would say because if we did, we would get boils on the butt. We then grew up and realised that it wasn't exactly boils they were trying to protect us from, but death itself. Why did I say this? While this is not exactly what happened with Adam and Eve, it is similar.

The only difference is that Adam and Eve died, spiritually. So, by choosing against God, by choosing to eat from the tree of the knowledge of good and evil – being like gods, Adam and Eve essentially chose to be independent of God. [John 10:34, Psalms 82:6] They made the same choice Satan made. And like Satan, they were spiritually dead – separated from God. We will talk more about this in later chapters.

So why did Satan do this? The fall of man did not benefit him in any way directly. The result was man's alienation with the creator, his curse and also resulted in the serpent receiving a curse. This was a significant battle in Satan's war against God. After his fall, the devil has was and has been on a mission to rebel against God. Man was living his purpose and was receiving instructions from God and was tempted into deciding good and evil on his own.  Satan, in the garden of Eden, Satan had his first *belligerents.* That is how this proxy war between God and Satan began.

Man exercised his agency and disobeyed God. As a result, he spiritually died – became separated from God. Man had chosen to decide on his own. He was banished from the garden of Eden and he had no access to the tree of life. That is how mortal death came to have power over him. What an anti-climax. The great creation story ended this way? Not at all.

It is interesting to note how man's life drastically changed from the moment he ate of the forbidden fruit. All of a sudden, he realises he was naked and he was ashamed of the fact. From the moment they were created, Adam and Eve never noticed this. They only notice it after eating the fruit.

This passage is both literal and prophetic. In the literal sense, it confirms that clothing yourself up is a good thing. Why? The tree that they ate from was the tree of the knowledge of both good and evil, not evil only. So they knew what was good and what was evil after eating of the fruit. Now, Scripture speaks of something fundamental about sin.

*[James 4:17] Therefore, to one who knows the right thing to do and does not do it, to him it is sin. NASB*

So, Adam and Eve realised the good that they had not clothed themselves in – obeying God and his following His lead. This is what made them feel ashamed

*[Isaiah 59:6] Their webs will not become clothing, nor will they cover themselves with their works; their works are works of iniquity, and an act of violence is in their hands. NASB*

*[Isaiah 61:10] I will greatly rejoice in the Lord, my soul shall be joyful in my God; for He has clothed me with the garments of salvation, He has covered me with the robe of righteousness, as a bridegroom decks himself with ornaments, and as a bride adorns herself with her jewels. NASB*

As highlighted by the two previous scriptures, in the bible, garments are symbolic of righteousness and evil alike. Righteousness is symbolized by clean garments while evil is symbolized by dirty garments.

*[Zechariah 3:1-5] Then he showed me Joshua the high priest standing before the angel of the Lord, and Satan standing at his right hand to accuse him. [2] The Lord said to Satan, "The Lord rebuke you, Satan! Indeed, the Lord who has chosen Jerusalem rebuke you! Is this not a brand plucked from the fire?" [3] Now Joshua was clothed with filthy garments and standing before the angel. [4] He spoke and said to those who were standing before him, saying, "Remove the filthy garments from*

*him." Again he said to him, "See, I have taken your iniquity away from you and will clothe you with festal robes."* [5] *Then I said, "Let them put a clean turban on his head." So put a clean turban on his head and clothed him with garments, while the angel of the Lord was standing by.*

Adam and Eve found themselves naked, not clothed by anything – neither righteousness nor evil.  And they wanted to cover themselves, which they did. The bible says they went and sewed together fig leaves and covered themselves. This was not effective and God had to clothe them with animal skin [Gen 3:21]. The prophetic significance of this act was that it symbolised the atonement later to come. An animal had to be killed and blood had to be shed for their covering. In the fullness of time, God Himself would send His son to die for man for his redemption. To clothe man in festal robes – righteousness.

The next thing man does is to distance Himself from God. Adam and Eve then hid from God because of the shame and the guilt. And it was God who looked for them, not the other way round. Adam then started making excuses, blaming God. Is it not interesting that this is the same thing that happens to us. Our sin makes us feel unworthy and we run away from God because of that. But then, there are only fig leaves away from God. Many times I have heard people indirectly blaming God for their shortcomings.

Many people love hiding behind the fact that God is omniscient, omnipotent and therefore is the cause of everything that we do or that happens to us. Dead wrong. God created us as free moral agents and has given us the dignity of causality. We live in a world where he gave jurisdiction to us and we are responsible for our actions – good or bad.

God then pronounces judgement on the serpent, the devil behind the serpent, Eve and also Adam. Yet, again He makes another prophetic statement regarding the future of man and His redemptive plan.

*[Genesis 3:15] And I will put enmity between you and the woman, and between your offspring and hers; he will crush your head, and you will strike his heel." NIV*

God declares enmity between the woman (the human race) and the serpent(the devil) and between the woman's seed and the devil's seed (rendered offspring in some versions). This seed or offspring pointed ultimately to Jesus Christ who was to come and destroy the works of the enemy. [1 John 3:8]

*[Galatians 3:6] Now the promises were spoken to Abraham and to his seed. He does not say, "And to seeds," as referring to many, but rather to one, "And to your seed," that is, Christ. NASB*

After this, man was banished from Eden and had to live off the land. One of the major reasons why He was banished from the garden was that God did not want our first parents to have access to the tree of life. [Gen 3:22]. So mortal death then followed. He would gradually return to the dust by the course of nature.

Adam and Even then live off the garden and they start the mission of multiplication. They then have their first child, Cain and then Abel. In the Christian circles, there has been discussion concerning how man multiplies. Not the physical act but what happens when a new human is conceived.

To understand why there has been a debate over this, we, once again, need to establish something fundamental. From the previous chapters, we have established that man's body was formed from the dust of the earth. We also established that man has a nonphysical part which distinguishes him from every other beast. Stopping here is quite easy and makes Christianity so easy but, it isn't. So, We won't stop here.

*[1 Thessalonians 5:23] "Now may the God of peace Himself sanctify you entirely; and may your spirit and soul and body be preserved complete, without blame at the coming of our Lord Jesus Christ." And may your whole spirit, soul, and body be kept sound and blameless at the coming of our Lord Jesus Christ." NASB*

*[Heb 4:12] For the word of God is living and active and sharper than any two-edged sword, and piercing as far as the division of soul and spirit, of both joints and*

The Apostle Paul confirms in his first letter to the Thessalonians that we indeed have a physical body. This is quite clear. He then goes further and explains in detail, the nonphysical part of our whole being. In his letter to the Hebrews, he makes clear that there is a distinction between the components that make our nonphysical part. There is what is called the soul, and what is called the spirit. These are distinct. So, man is tripartite. Man has a body, a soul and a spirit.

I must stress that this is not the Apostle's idea. From [Genesis 2:7], we see man's body is formed from the dust of the earth then we see God breathing into his nostrils and man became a living soul. So the union of the body from below and the spirit from above gave birth to a living soul – a living personality.

Physically, there are parts of our bodies that we cannot even see. No man can see his back without the use of a mirror. We use the mirror to be able to see some of our body parts. It is essentially the same as our nonphysical selves. We need a spiritual mirror to be able to understand who we are and what exactly are we made of. It is only the word of God that can divide the soul from the spirit.

*[James 1:23-24] For if anyone is a hearer of the word and not a doer, he is like a man who looks at his natural face in a mirror; for once he has looked at himself and*

*gone away, he has immediately forgotten what kind of person he was. NASB*

The word of God is the mirror that can help us understand man. It has been a paradox from ages past. There have been lots of studies to establish what man is and many have fallen short. Even the man after God's own heart was intrigued by the idea of man and who he was. [Psalms 8:4-8]

Going back to the account of creation, it will be useful to use the original Hebrew and Greek text used for the body, soul and spirit so that we can better understand.

Hebrew:

Spirit – Ruach: Meaning a self-existent, continuous life-giving force.  The spirit came from God and is the life-giving force.

*[1 Cor 15:45] So also it is written, "The first MAN, Adam, BECAME A LIVING SOUL." The last Adam became a life-giving spirit. NASB*

Soul – Nephesh: Signifying taking in a breath and giving it out. The soul has to receive life to live. The spirit has life and is life.

Greek:

Spirit – Pneuma: meaning wind or breath. Signifying that it was breathed in

Soul – Psyche: Meaning the human soul or the mind

We had talked about the fall of man. And we established that his disobedience to the command of God led to his death – spiritual death. Man spiritually died. i.e he was separated from the life of God. Man's soul became corrupted from the rebellion. Initially, man had to be tempted from outside. That is why the devil had to come in the form of a serpent to tempt man. But now, after the fall, man knew evil and could be tempted from within. From that, he became corrupt in his soul. By nature, corruption is progressive. It starts slowly unto full corruption.

Man's body became corrupt as well and would deteriorate until his physical death.

Remember this definition of man started from the need to understand Creationism and Traducionism. Traducionism is the scripture-backed idea that when humans reproduce, the reproduce a complete man – body, soul and spirit. Creationists believe that each time a woman conceives, their spirit comes from God. I have to categorically state that nothing from scripture has given me any strong inclination to creationism. What this view fails to explain is why man is corrupt from birth and why man would need regeneration.

So, Adam and Eve, following the command to multiply and to replenish the earth, they had children after their kind. The general principle of a seed is that it produces after its kind. A mango seed will always produce a mango tree. They gave birth to Cain and Abel. Reading from the book of Genesis (Chapter 4), we understand that Cain went on to kill Abel. He was corrupt from birth and the corruption was progressive. And so was Abel.

This continued with the passing generation and humanity became even more corrupt. We read of Noah's flood again in the book of Genesis. Sodom and Gomorrah, the Nazi concentration camps at Auschwitz et cetera. In a nutshell, man is born corrupt. I was born corrupt, dead in my trespasses and separated from God. And so were you.

# Chapter Five

Regeneration

All hope is not lost. In his corruption and his independence from God, man has done and continues to wreak havoc upon the earth, harm his fellow humans and above all, is even a slave to himself. Created to be God's vice-regent on earth, he is a slave to his desires and can't even rule his own body. Man has invented a lot of things to try and fill the void he has but all of it comes short. All of it is meaningless away from God.

Over two thousand years ago, God Himself came down on earth in the person of Jesus Christ of Nazareth, just as it had been prophetically promised from Genesis and by the prophets of the old covenant. He came to pay for the sin of the world and to redeem mankind from corruption. He came to reconcile humanity to God. To give life to the dead spirit and reconnect it back to God.

This is where regeneration comes into play. Regeneration is the only way through which man can be saved and in the next paragraphs, I will explain how it happens in simple terms.

Regeneration happens from a seed. And the seed is the word of God. [Luke 8:11]

*[11] "Now the parable is this: the seed is the word of God. [12] Those beside the road are those who have*

*heard; then the devil comes and takes away the word from their heart, so that they will not believe and be saved. <sup>13</sup> Those on the rocky soil are those who, when they hear, receive the word with joy; and these have no firm root; they believe for a while, and in time of temptation fall away. <sup>14</sup> The seed which fell among the thorns, these are the ones who have heard, and as they go on their way they are choked with worries and riches and pleasures of this life, and bring no fruit to maturity. <sup>15</sup> But the seed in the good soil, these are the ones who have heard the word in an honest and good heart, and hold it fast, and bear fruit with perseverance .NASB*

When man hears the word of God, is convicted of his rebellion by the Holy Spirit and receives the spoken word with faith, he receives the seed of regeneration. It then takes a supernatural act of the Holy Spirit to make the seed germinate. The seed may have latent potential in it but it has to be realised.

*[John 3:6] <sup>6</sup> That which is born of the flesh is flesh, and that which is born of the Spirit is spirit. NASB*

Notice that scripture says that which is born of the Spirit (capital S) is spirit. So then man's spirit is reborn and is brought back into communion with the father.

*[1 Corinthians 6:17] <sup>17</sup> But the one who joins himself to the Lord is one spirit with Him. NASB*

Notice that it is the spirit, not the soul that is made one with God. The soul is saved from the penalty of sin – death and the body is quickened from this new life.

# Chapter Six

## The War

So the born again Christian is the one whose spirit has been regenerated. Jesus tells Nicodemus that it is impossible for a man to enter the kingdom of God unless he is born of water and the Spirit. [John 3:5]. Regeneration is the only way through which man can be reconciled back to God.

Regeneration creates a completely new spirit which has the perfect image of God in a man. Thus when a man is born again, he is a new creature.

*[2 Cor 5:17][17] Therefore if anyone is in Christ, he is a new creature; the old things passed away; behold, new things have come. NASB*

But his soul is still corrupt. It is his spirit that is completely new. His body is also still subject to corruption. This creates a conflict within man. His spirit is reconnected to God and is God-conscious but, his soul, from the corruption, is self-conscious and his body is world conscious. The components of his complete being are in a state of war.

*[Galatians 5:17] For the flesh sets its desire against the Spirit, and the Spirit against the flesh; for these are in opposition to one another, so that you may not do the things that you please. NASB*

It is important to note that the soul and the body from the modern translations of the bible are most times referred to as the flesh. So whenever you see the word flesh in the bible it sometimes refers to the body or the body and the soul.

Let's look into the functions of the spirit, soul and body.

Spirit – God-conscious

1. Worship: [John 4:23]. Worship is the regenerated spirit's response to the one and true God to which it was reconnected.

2. Fellowship: [1 Cor 14:2]. If you remember from the garden of Eden, man would fellowship with God. Fellowship is the highest expression of friendship between God and man. It is in fellowship that God reveals His secrets to man. It was after fellowship that God revealed His plans to destroy Sodom and Gomorrah to Abraham. [Genesis 18]

3. Revelation: The spirit receives information from God. Revelation is the function of the spirit. [Rev 1:1-9]. The spirit has a direct knowledge of God. It just knows.

4. The spirit is constant because it receives from God who is unchanging. [Mal 3:6]

The Soul – Self Conscious

The soul is the self, the ego. It is the centre of the three important faculties of decision making.

1. Will – Man is a free moral agent with a will. The human will directs what decision a man makes. All statements that start with 'I will' are expressions of the Will.

2. Intellect – Man's ability to think rationally. The soul, via the intellect, plays around with ideas and concepts, weighing them until it finds the most likely to take. Theology is in this realm. The spirit has revelation.

3. Emotions – Our emotions respond to impressions from the intellect or the body. Emotions are not constant. They change every time because their source is in constant change

Praise is a function of the soul. Praise is appreciation. The soul praises expressing appreciation.

The body – World conscious

1. The body receives information and stimuli from the physical world. It is the realm of the senses. It receives and they are processed in the mind.

2. The body expresses impressions of the mind or the spirit. It is with the body that we talk, walk or do anything physical which is an expression of the mind's will or decision.

3. The body is the temple of God. It is the avenue via which God works in the physical world. [Lev 26:11]

The ideal Christian

Just like before the fall, the ideal man should be led by God. God gave us an example of operation in His image in Jesus Christ – truly man and truly God. [Col 1:15-18]. Because the spirit of man receives from God, it is designed to control and lead the soul and the soul controls and directs the body. That means the intended man should operate fully on the direction of God Himself.

The born Again Christian

The born again Christian finds himself in a state of war. A situation in which his spirit is receiving instruction from God but his soul has different ideas. From the corruption of ages, he is tempted every day by his desires from within his soul. [James 1:4]

His body and senses receive information and stimuli that suggest decisions that are in contrast to what his spirit receives from God. His soul finds itself being a battleground. It is a constant fight every single day of his life until he is conformed to the exact image of Christ.

*[Proverbs 4:18] But the path of the righteous is like the light of dawn, That shines brighter and brighter until the full day. NASB*

*[Romans 12:2] And do not be conformed to this world, but be transformed by the renewing of your mind, so*

*that you may prove what the will of God is, that which is good and acceptable and perfect. NASB*

From the day man is born, the corruption in him starts progressing. He learns a lot of things from his environment and he discovers his inclination to doing bad. From being an innocent toddler he grows into a wicked, misinformed adult, prone to doing evil, independent from his source of life and in need of a saviour.

When he receives the saviour, the war begins. Because in him, he has a perfect new creature (his spirit) and an old and wicked soul. To add to that, he also has a body that is world conscious. The apostle Paul acknowledging this wrote to the Romans and instructed them not to be conformed to this world but to be transformed.

There is a transformation of man's soul that has to happen and it is not an overnight experience. A good example of this is what I saw the other time when the council had to change a sewer system. They did not take out all the pipes completely but replaced an old piece one by one until all of it was new. Also bear in mind that it took more than a day for man's corruption to develop. It takes time, and so does the unlearning. It is a process of unlearning all the bad information and replacing it with the new and perfect. Until man reflects the perfect image of Christ.

And the devil, our adversary, knowing this, capitalises on man's corruption to bring him down again as he did in the garden. Remember there was enmity sworn between the woman's seed and his seed.

Back to our second anchor text:

*[2 Cor 10:3-5]. For though we live in the world, we do not wage war as the world does. The weapons we fight with are not the weapons of the world. On the contrary, they have divine power to demolish strongholds. We demolish arguments and every pretension that sets itself up against the knowledge of God, and we take captive every thought to make it obedient to Christ. NIV*

# Chapter Seven

The Enemy's Kingdom

From our first anchor text:

*[Eph 6:12] For our struggle is not against flesh and blood, but against the rulers, against the powers, against the world forces of this darkness, against the spiritual forces of wickedness in the heavenly places. NASB*

We must understand that the devil has a kingdom that is well structured. And this is not because of his genius but it is simply because he was cast out of heaven, a perfect kingdom with structures therefore, he had seen this somewhere.  When he was cast out of heaven, there was a third of the angels that were in heaven that had joined him in his rebellion against God and were cast away together with him. [Rev 12:4, Rev 12:9]

Together, they form a kingdom with descending orders or authority and these different ranks have jurisdiction over areas and subareas.

From [Genesis 1:1], we understand that in the beginning, God created the *heavens* and the earth. Heavens is plural and signifies that there is more than one heaven. Let us look at more scripture.

*[2 Cor 12:2] I know a man in Christ who fourteen years ago-- whether in the body I do not know, or out of the*

*body I do not know, God knows-- such a man was caught up to the third heaven. NASB*

The Apostle Paul mentioned a man who was caught up in the third heaven. There has never been a third of anything without the first and the second. This is from pure logic. This information implies that there are at least three heavens.

More scripture again, lest we build a doctrine from one verse.

*[Eph 4:10] He who descended is Himself also He who ascended far above all the heavens, so that He might fill all things.) NASB*

The first heaven is the atmosphere that we see. It is the sky and where birds fly.

[Matt 6:36] Look at the birds of the air, for they neither sow nor reap nor gather in barns; yet your heavenly Father feeds them. NASB

The Greek word for air is *Ouranos*, which can be translated to heaven. E.g in

*[James 5:18] And he [Elijah] prayed again, and the heaven gave rain, and the earth produced fruit.*

Supporting scripture: [Deut 11:17, Deut 28:12, Judges 5:4, Acts 14:17]

Then there is the second heaven, sometimes called the celestial heaven or the stellar heaven. This is where the sun, moon and stars are. [Isa 13:10, Jer 8:2, Ps 19:4, Deut 17:3]

*[Mathew 24:29] Immediately after the tribulation of those days the sun will be darkened, and the moon will not give its light; the stars will fall from heaven, and the powers of the heavens will be shaken. KJV*

Then there is the third heaven, where God dwells. The heaven of heavens.

*[Deut 10:14] Indeed heaven and the highest heavens belong to the Lord your God, also the earth with all that is in it. KJV*

It is the throne of God and it is where God dwells. It is Paradise.

*2 Chr 2:6: But who is able to build him a house, seeing the heaven and heaven of heavens cannot contain him? Who am I then, that I should build him an house, save only to burn sacrifice before him? KJV*

It is also important to note that God is not limited by geographical space.

The Kingdom of the devil operates from the second heaven. It is from where principalities and powers of this dark age wage war. In the book of Daniel, [Daniel 10:13], we understand that after praying, Daniel's request was heard and his answer was given. However, the angel who was sent to deliver the message was resisted by the prince of Persia for 21 days until an angel of higher rank, Michael, had to come and fight on his behalf. The angel also then mentions that he was going again to fight the prince of Persia on his way.

Let us understand what was happening in this passage. Daniel went on a fast for three weeks on account of the suffering of his people, the people of Israel, under bondage by the king of Persia. After three weeks of fasting, Daniel then sees an angel who came with a message from God. The angel then reveals that he had been resisted for 21 days by the prince of Persia in the heavenly realm. The physical king of Persia was Cyrus and was ruling over an approximate 127 provinces here on earth. But angel Gabriel is fought by the prince of Persia, a spiritual force and authority.

This takes us back to [Isaiah 14] where the king of Babylon was addressed but also, the devil who was working behind the physical king of Babylon. It also takes us back to [Ezekiel 28] where the prince of Tyre is addressed, as well as the devil who was behind the prince of Tyre. For geographical spaces here on earth, there are territorial spirits that are assigned. They are in a hierarchy and they are assigned over areas and subareas depending on the hierarchy.

The angel Gabriel then goes on to mention that the archangel Michael, the angel of Israel, fights for Gabriel against these principalities. So these principalities influence what happens in this physical realm. These principalities have foot soldiers under their command that are called demons.

*[Mathew 12:25] Then a demon-possessed man who was blind and mute was brought to Jesus, and He healed him, so that the mute man spoke and saw. All the crowds were amazed, and were saying, "This man cannot be the Son of David, can he?" But when the Pharisees heard this, they said, "This man casts out demons only by Beelzebul the ruler of the demons." And knowing their thoughts Jesus said to them, "Any kingdom divided against itself is laid waste; and any city or house divided against itself will not stand. "If Satan casts out Satan, he is divided against himself; how then will his kingdom stand? "If I by Beelzebul cast out demons, by whom do your sons cast them out? For this reason they will be your judges. "But if I cast out demons by the Spirit of God, then the kingdom of God has come upon you. "Or how can anyone enter the strong man's house and carry off his property, unless he first binds the strong man? And then he will plunder his house. NASB*

Our Lord Jesus in this portion of scripture reveals important information. He first reveals that the devil has a kingdom and it has superior ranks and inferior ranks – demons. As I said, demons belong in the kingdom of the devil and they are the foot soldiers. Demons were not part of the third of angels cast out of heaven. They are of a different origin which is not the thrust of this book. Their origin is covered in demonology. In this book, we are interested in how they implement their master's strategy on earth.

Now we have established that the devil has a kingdom in which he is the king. His kingdom is organised in hierarchies and has authorities that rule over territories as well as foot soldiers. Now, there is a strategy of waging this war.

The Enemy's strategy

Once again I will remind you of the statement made by the author of the book "The art of war"

*"All warfare is based on deception. Hence, when we are able to attack, we must seem unable; when using our forces, we must appear inactive; when we are near, we must make the enemy believe we are far away; when far away, we must make him believe we are near."*
*— Sun Tzu, The Art of War*

All warfare is based on deception. I have found this statement to be true on many fronts. This is not the only strategy but it is one of the oldest in the playbook. And it works most times. It worked on our first parents – Adam and Eve.

The devil has been in the business of deceiving people from the beginning. The bible calls him the father of lies. His end goal is preventing regeneration, sabotaging it or making it ineffective. One of the many reasons why he does it is I believe is to prove to God that man is wicked, needs independence from God and only worships God because he is scared of losing out on the good things from God. At the heart of it all, the devil stands for independence from God. Doing as you please and being your boss. We see a classic example of this in the first chapter of the book of Job. [Job 1]

The deception is quite structured that you would believe. And the one thing that makes it work is the principle stated by Sun Tzu. When the devil influences us into making a decision we think it is entirely ourselves and when he is not even directly in the picture, we spend nights binding and casting. This is exactly how the devil works.

[2 Cor 2:11] [11] *so that no advantage would be taken of us by Satan, for we are not ignorant of his schemes. NASB*

## Strongholds

The devil operates on schemes, which by definition, are large-scale systematic plans. Like it or not, I believe there are long term plans the devil puts in motion that will work for a very long time. They take a long time to put into place but they are highly effective when they start to work.

[2 Cor 10:3-5] highlights something important. It mentions that our weapons have divine power enough to demolish strongholds. Strongholds, in literal army terms, are fortresses, places fortified for security against attacks. A fortress can be a place of refuge [Psalms 9:9] or it can be a place where an enemy attacks from, making it difficult to overpower the enemy.

In spiritual terms, strongholds are ideas and thoughts that take root in a person's life and form a framework of reference in them. They form the basis on which one sees the world and interpret events around them. Strongholds include ideas about God, ideas about life and ideas about yourself as an individual. These ideas usually are developed over time. From the time a person is born until they die.

## The Environment

Many things shape the development of strongholds in one's life. A person born today in Chitungwiza, Zimbabwe will have a lot of factors shaping his ideas about life. The fact that he is in Africa is a contributor on its own. He may be proud of the beautiful weather, flora and fauna in Africa but, he will also remember the fact that the first time Africans met the European and American races, his race was enslaved. The second time it was slavery. This may sound like bringing up the past but, it will take a lot of learning and a lot of experiences for someone to believe in their heart that they are created equal with anyone else from any other race. This is the reason why Moses had to stress the fact that man was created in God's image. Why? When the children of Israel were slaves in Egypt, they were told that only the Pharaoh was created in the image of God and hence could and was supposed to rule over them. It then would become a challenge for them to establish nations and empires without a reconditioning. The word of God had to transform their minds according to the truth. It was a very liberating truth to know that they too, just like the Pharaohs were created in the same image, the image of God.

It is no different in the case of a child who is born in Africa. That is the first stronghold that limits him. Even from the categorisation of the world, he is born in the third world. And some are born in the first. If this person is born again, they will need the word of God again to pull this stronghold down. Unless this is done, this person will never feel confident enough to compete at anything against anyone from the first world. On the other hand, the one in the first world, particularly from a great nation like the United States, will more likely feel superior to anyone from the third world. This creates what is generally called the superiority complex and the inferiority complex.

I also believe that inasmuch as it has to become a renewal of the mind, in the realm of the spirit, there are principalities that are responsible for enforcing these complexes. In turn, they have foot soldiers that can be assigned to enforce these lies. We have already seen that the devil can influence physical people to behave or act in a certain way.

National pride does the same to the mentality of a person as well. This is not something that started in this generation.

*[Judges 6:15] He said to Him, "O Lord, how shall I deliver Israel? Behold, my family is the least in Manasseh, and I am the youngest in my father's house." NASB*

When God was sending Gideon to deliver Israel, he had to deal with his inferiority complex. From his ideology of life, only the bigger tribes like Judah were meant to do this type of task. He was limited at what he could achieve because of his tribe. It did not take only the word of an angel, it had to take a test. He wanted God to prove that He would indeed be with him on this feat.

It is the same with many people today. It takes some evidence to convince them that they are equally capable and competent. Sometimes it takes the success of a fellow third world citizen to convince others that they too can rise above their circumstances. This is the first stronghold that one has to realise and conquer. It is also important for anyone coming from a country with great pride to regard other people as second class citizens. This is the root of pride and prejudice. The problem with this is that they stop you from learning or benefitting from anything that could come from the 'inferior' nationalities or tribes.

Then being Zimbabwean will shape his ideas about certain things differently from how someone born in South Africa will develop their idea of the same thing. At the time of writing, Zimbabwe has had only two presidents. Depending on perspective, any person can conclude the legacies left by the two presidents. If one focuses on the weaknesses of the two presidents, it is very easy for any to believe that bad leadership is God's will. Wherever it is, an oppressive regime will always instil fear in its citizens. Throughout history, people that have tried to rise against oppressive governments and have been butchered or imprisoned may inspire some but, most times become an example of what not to do. This produces a group of people that is so docile and keeps quiet whenever they are oppressed. It is different from country to country.

The next thing that will shape the young man's mind is the city and neighbourhood he is born in. Chitungwiza is not the best suburb in Harare so another possible inferiority complex is developed with regards others from the northern suburbs of Harare – where the rich and powerful usually stay. Chitungwiza, being a high-density suburb, has a lot of dynamics in it. Normally there is a type of music that is prevalent in these suburbs. Some of it pure but much of it promotes drug abuse and promiscuity. Not saying this music is not common in the low-density suburbs. It is there but the difference is that it is very hard to develop a taste in music, in the ghetto, without being influenced by society. People stay close together and kids grow up playing street football together and going to the same schools.

Then it trickles down to family. The family dynamic is one of the most important ones. The family set up plays a major part in shaping the soul of a person. The fact that we refer to God as our father is significant. A person will always try to relate, at first, God to their earthly father. If you grew up in a home where the father is almost only the guy to which all your mischief is escalated then you will always see God as an angry God who is holding a whip at you all the time, tracking all your movements to punish your mistakes. It will equally be hard for you to imagine a relationship with God if you never had a relationship with your earthly father.

In a nutshell, a person's environment will create strongholds in their minds – their souls. When one then is born again, it becomes difficult to reconcile their soulish knowledge and spiritual truths. Now, some of the things are out of anyone's control, like where one is born. Some people are just born in countries that are Muslim and they become Muslim. Likewise, some people are born in nations where Christianity is the prevalent religion and they become Christian. This is not to say any religion is right because it is socially influenced. I got to a point where I had some confusion about this. The devil was using this to fight my faith but, thank God for His Holy Spirit and His Word that is the truth that sets free. [John 8:32]. I will shed some light on this issue in the subsequent passages. Some of the environmental factors are within man's control – parents' control. The family environment is the responsibility of every parent and unknowingly, many parents have created toxic environments for their children by their behaviour. Some of the behaviour is influenced by the devil and devils. The enemy is much active on this one. He has made many men reject their babies or families to create an environment of bitterness and one in which children grow up with no direction and without a father figure. In the end, we have young women dating older men for money and young men abusing women because they never had an example of a man loving his woman.

The family institution is the one that has been attacked in this age because it has power to shape individuals, societies and in turn, nations and the world.

    A. <u>Information</u>
       i) <u>Education</u>

The other thing that will shape a person's framework of reference is information. Education is one sphere that is largely responsible for informing individuals. From elementary school to college, it is information on different levels. Much of the information disseminated at the higher education levels can be detrimental. I have heard people who say the more education you get, the more you are likely not to believe in God. It is not a surprise that most educated people feel they are much more enlightened for church et cetera. I was almost caught in this trap myself. What happens is that with more education, you equip your soul (mind) with information. This information could be an opinion and some could be the truth so, without the real truth of the word of God pulling it down, it becomes an enemy of God. It is good to learn Darwinian evolution for the sake of knowledge but this can easily lead someone into being a naturalist. That is why the Apostle John [3 John 1:2] wished that the church prospers in all things (including spiritual things) just as the soul prospers.

In Moses' time, there were several stories and legends about the origin of man and the earth.  Just like there are stories about creation today. Different theories of the big bang and evolution. That was why Moses, by revelation, wrote authoritatively in the first book of the bible. In the beginning, God created the heavens and the earth. He was addressing such lies that confused people. To every man, it is clear that something not human created the universe and the devil tries to deceive people in this regard. The devil wants mankind to believe that we originated from something impersonal that doesn't have demands on our beings.

For Christians, this is not a big issue. The most appealing lie on the market sold by the devil is dualism. The devil has managed to convince some Christians that he is an equal and opposite power to God. But from the account of the Bible, he is a created being. The devil is not another evil god who wages war against a good God. Satan is a fallen angel, who deceives.

From a logical standpoint, here is how dualism fails. If there are two powers, one called good and the other called bad, it must follow that the other simply likes goodness for goodness sake and the other likes badness for badness sake. But then, no one really likes evil for the sake of liking evil. From our experience, people do bad things to get good things. The good things can be riches or money. People can kill for money. Not because money is bad but because it is good. On the other hand, people can be kind for the sake of being kind. People can love for the sake of love. So in essence, evil cannot even exist without good. But good can exist on its own.

The other pertinent fact to note is that the moment we say a power is good and another is bad, we are implying the existence of a standard of good that we measure these powers against. And who would be this standard? Where would the standard of good come from unless there is another impersonation of good that is beyond the two powers in comparison? In a nutshell, dualism fails dismally. And this is one powerful truth the Christian must know. The Bible says that the world will be shocked when it finally realises who Satan is, a created being who roars like a lion but is not even one. The world will be surprised to know that nations were shaken by a powerless being. [Isaiah 14:16]

### ii)  <u>Media and the Internet</u>

This generation has access to the internet ad it is even another challenge inasmuch as it is a blessing. Instant fact-checking is a good idea but there is a caveat, much of today's journalism and publishing is propaganda and clickbait. Almost every article, song, video or movie has an agenda or some undertone to it.

Yes, some art is a pure expression or pure storytelling but, much of the information as agendas and undertones. The information that one has access to can shape how they think and ultimately who they are. As a man thinks in his heart, so is he. [Proverbs 23:7].

It is easy for a person to get addicted to pornography because they first heard that masturbation is healthy from some health expert. Yes, there will be biological facts to support the claim but the born again Christian must not be addicted to anything except God Himself.

There are principalities and demons that are responsible for the dissemination of information. We must understand that the devil is not omnipresent. He is very limited in his ability as well as resources. Because of this, his attacks and schemes are well calculated. In [Isaiah 14] and [Ezekiel 28] the devil did not influence an average person. He had to influence the king of Babylon and the prince of Tyre. It was a well-calculated move. Influencing the kings would, in turn, influence the entire society. Kings were in positions of power and influence over all their subjects. They would declare a thing and it would be so. We read of King Nebuchadnezzar [Daniel 1-4], a Babylonian king who built a statue and commanded everyone to worship it. He is not the one referred to in Isaiah 14 but, this is just to highlight the influence these Babylonian kings had.

This was exactly why the devil influenced the kings. Whatever he would push through the kings would be propagated down to the masses. It is the same today. In a nation, the devil will target the most influential voices and try to influence a lot of people via these proxies. In today's world presidents are not the only influential people around. Different voices become authorities in their fields of expertise and they become the devil's target.

If one newspaper article can be read by millions of people, I'm sure the devil would want to influence that newspaper. If a tweet can reach billions of people then I believe the devil would want to influence that account. If one song can reach over a billion ears then I believe the devil would want to promote lust or violence through it. There are respected voices (in all spheres of society – media, politics, education, entertainment etc.) in the world that, if influenced by the devil, become the very mouthpiece of the devil himself.

The misunderstood part about this is that these voices, many times, do not even know the influence of the devil on their lives. Most times they think it is themselves and their minds only.

The Apostle Peter was once under the influence of the devil and was not even aware.

*[Mathew 16:21 -23] From that time Jesus began to show His disciples that He must go to Jerusalem, and suffer many things from the elders and chief priests and scribes, and be killed, and be raised up on the third day. Peter took Him aside and began to rebuke Him, saying, "God forbid it, Lord! This shall never happen to You." But He turned and said to Peter, "Get behind Me, Satan! You are a stumbling block to Me; for you are not setting your mind on God's interests, but man's." NASB*

The very purpose of the coming of Christ was to redeem mankind. He was to become the sacrifice for sin. Our Lord Jesus then began telling His disciples that He had to go through these things and the devil tries to abort that mission by influencing Peter. And note that the devil behind Peter did not come directly against God's plan but he came from a humanitarian angle. It would appear to be that Peter was so concerned about the welfare of Jesus but in fact, the devil was coming against the redemption plan.

Many plans have been aborted because of 'being human'. Much discussion on demonization will follow in the upcoming chapters.

iii) <u>Religion</u>

Religion is another pillar of society that is capable of informing and also misinforming a person. The devil has crept into the church and there are doctrines of devils(1 Tim 4:1) that are circulating that sound so logical and sound spiritual when they are lies from hell, meant to derail unsuspecting religious people.

False doctrines are some of the most difficult strongholds to deal with because they are sometimes based on scripture itself.

Here are some of the reasons why there are false doctrines and heretic beliefs out there.

Inaccurate Understanding of Covenants: The Bible is God's inspired word. It is divided into two covenants/testaments – The Old Testament and the New Testament. The former contains the history of the earth and mankind from Genesis. It also details how tribes and nations came to be and in particular, it narrates the fall of man and the planned rescue plan in the books of the prophets. God entered into a covenant first with Abraham, then affirmed the covenant with Isaac and Jacob and then re-affirmed it with Moses [Exodus 19 – 24]. A saviour was promised to come and redeem mankind from the fall.

The New Testament/covenant begins when the promised saviour Jesus dies for mankind and redeems it. From the death of Jesus, the New covenant kicks in and is a dispensation of Grace from the death and resurrection of the Messiah, with the Holy Spirit being the guide, teacher and comforter. The Old Covenant was a covenant of the law. I will not dwell much on the differences between the covenants but one fact that is essential to know is this: You and I live in the new testament and the way we relate to God is different from the way the children of Israel related to God in the Old Testament.

So, today, there will still be Christians trying to relate to God according to how the children of Israel related to Him in the Old Testament. This has been a major source of differences between doctrines in the body of Christ and has been a stronghold in the majority of religious minds. The Old Testament, being based on law, was a legalistic covenant. While the New Testament, which is based on Grace, does not promote sin, it preaches salvation by grace and not works. I am not here to explicitly command you what you choose to believe but I am here to highlight that you need to understand the differences in the covenants at a personal level. Some of the strongholds in your life are a result of an erroneous interpretation of the two covenants in the Bible. So in as much as the Old and New testaments are parts of the Bible, they have to be interpreted differently.

Building doctrines without supporting Scripture:

*[1 Cor 14: 26 – 33] What is the outcome then, brethren? When you assemble, each one has a psalm, has a teaching, has a revelation, has a tongue, has an interpretation. Let all things be done for edification. If anyone speaks in a tongue, it should be by two or at the most three, and each in turn, and one must interpret; but if there is no interpreter, he must keep silent in the church; and let him speak to himself and to God. Let two or three prophets speak, and let the others pass judgment. But if a revelation is made to another who is seated, the first one must keep silent. For you can all prophesy one by one, so that all may learn and all may be exhorted; and the spirits of prophets are subject to prophets; for God is not a God of confusion but of peace, as in all the churches of the saints. NASB*

The Apostle Paul when he was addressing the Corinthian church instructed the prophets to agree on whatever they heard from God. If God spoke to one of the prophets, the other prophets had to confirm the message. If this was a duty then it is also a duty today. Throughout scripture, important themes and truths are supported by several verses and chapters. It is very easy to err if a doctrine is built on one verse. If the prophets could err, it is also possible for teachers and ministers to interpret scripture wrongly. Whichever doctrines you believe in, make sure you have thoroughly read about it and that it is supported not just by one out of 31,102 verses. It has to be backed by some scripture.

Eisegesis instead of Exegesis: Almost every seminary teaches on eisegesis and exegesis in a hermeneutics module. Exegesis is the reading of the scriptural text from the original context, to determine the accurate intent of the author. On the other hand, Eisegesis is about reading into the text with a preconceived notion. We view the world in different cultural lenses that are socially induced. It becomes a problem when we then start reading the word of God with these primitive cultural lenses and try to read our preconceived notions into the text.

This happens a lot in the Christian circles and has led to a wrong interpretation of the text. The example I gave of a child who grows in a dysfunctional family and under abuse from the father may often fail to understand the love of God the Father if he reads his notions about fathers into any biblical text.

It is imperative to drop these cultural lenses before reading the word of God. This is another stronghold in the lives of many people. Whenever they read the bible they end up seeing what they already think about the world and God and it is dangerous.

With all this said, It begins to shape up. We will still build on the case but right now, I think it is clear to see that many factors can lead to misinformation. This misinformation becomes a stronghold in one's life and has to be unlearnt over time. It's very easy to believe that it's only information that we have to change. This makes one fall into the devil's trap – thinking that he is not attacking when he is.

There are pastors and ministers in Christian circles who, either knowingly or unknowingly, are preaching false doctrines. The bible speaks of a time when people will surround themselves with preachers that will tell them what they want to hear.

*[2 Tim 4:3] For the time will come when they will not endure sound doctrine; but wanting to have their ears tickled, they will accumulate for themselves teachers in accordance to their own desires. NASB*

Ministry has become a career in this generation and just like in any profession, there are fakes and wolves out there. The devil has thrown some of these fakes into the Christian circles and they are spreading lies, telling people what they naturally want to hear and not the undiluted word of the cross. [Jer 23:32, Matt 24:11, Jer 23]

*[Matthew 24:24] "For false Christs and false prophets will arise and will show great signs and wonders, so as to mislead, if possible, even the elect. NASB*

The big problem in the church today is not sinning, but false teaching.

The problem with false teaching is that it gives people the wrong ideas about God most of the times. The problem with wrong interpretation of scripture (Eisegesis) is that it limits the Gospel, and sometimes it gives the completely wrong meaning of the text. There is prevalent legalistic teaching in many parts of Africa that makes people think they will earn heaven by their works. This belief takes root because of the continent's history of slavery.

There are lots of other doctrines that are pure heresy but are taught in some churches. They become a stronghold that sometimes limits people and enslaves them. If a Bible seminary teaches false doctrine, imagine the growth of that doctrine if that seminary churns out hundred ordained pastors in a year? The growth is exponential.

iv) <u>Experience</u>

There is a general belief that we are all the total of our experiences and it is true to a certain extent. There is a saying that goes 'experience is the greatest teacher'. It is a true saying but, the truth is, different experiences do not teach the same lesson. The way things happen to us can determine what we learn from each experience. The loss of a loved one can teach different things to different people in different circumstances.

A child who loses their only parent when all of their hope was in that parent may make them believe God does not even care about them. The loss is an experience but, what it may teach is not the truth. As we live, there are many statements thrown around by hurting people or misinformed people that, many times, we shove to the back of our minds and don't dwell on them much. But, sometimes, these are brought to the front of our minds when we have certain experiences.

You may hear a hurting person claiming God doesn't care and dismiss the thought altogether and move on with your life. When you then get into a situation in which you find yourself hurting, such claims rush back to your mind and all of a sudden you start entertaining the idea. You start pondering and sometimes you start connecting dots and it starts making sense. How quickly you conclude depends on how well you 'connect the dots' or the number of similar experiences.

Suppose this same child who loses their last parent looks forward to the extended family taking care of him, which they do not and he ends up in an orphanage somewhere. He starts connecting the dots and this time, with a second experience. A lot of similar experiences may happen to this child and with each experience, the idea that God does not care is reinforced in this child's mind.

In the end, he starts giving other people 'advice'. The problem with this type of deception is that it comes from 'many experiences'. When this child grows to forty or fifty and they get a chance to talk to a grieving child, they will say "You know what? I've been here before and I can tell you one thing, God doesn't care. " It is this 'advice' from hurting people or people that have been through the worst of things that you hear people giving on bar tables after glasses of whiskey or vodka.

A single mother who has had terrible experiences with absent fathers is more likely to have her girl children believe all men are trash as it's usually said.

This is not a completely new phenomenon. There is a man called Willie Lynch who was a slave owner and is infamous for his letter 'The making of a slave'.

In this letter to other slave owners, delivered on the Thames river in 1712, he outlines a peculiar method of breaking the negro to create a cycle that produces slaves from every generation with ease. For the full letter you can look for it on the internet but, below is an extract from the letter, which is the actual breaking of the negro.

*Take the meanest and most restless nigger, strip him of his clothes in front of the remaining male niggers, the female, the nigger infant, tar and feather him, tie each leg to a different horse in opposite directions, set him on fire and beat both horses to pull him apart in front of the remaining niggers. The next step is to take a bullwhip and beat the remaining nigger male to the point of death in front of the female and the infant. Don't kill him, but put the fear of God in him, for he can be useful for future breeding.*

*Then take the female and run a series of test on her to see if she will submit to your desire willingly. Test her in every way because she is the most important factor for good economics. If she shows any sign of resistance in submitting completely to your will, do not hesitate to use the bullwhip on her to extract the last bit of bi**h* *out of her. Take care not to kill her, for in doing so, you spoil good economics. When in complete submission, she will train her offspring in the early years to submit to labour when they become of age.*

*Understanding is the best thing. Therefore, we shall go deeper into this area of the subject matter concerning what we have produced here in this breaking process of the female nigger. We have reversed relationships. In her natural uncivilized state she would have a strong dependency on the uncivilized nigger male, and she would have a limited protective tendency toward her independent male offspring and would raise the female offspring to be dependent like her. Nature had provided time with this balance.*

*We reversed nature by burning and pulling one civilized nigger apart and bullwhipping the other to the point of death –all in her presence.*

*By her being left alone, unprotected, with the male image destroyed, the ordeal caused her to move from her psychologically dependent state to a frozen independent state. In this frozen psychological state of independence, she will raise her male and female offspring in reversed roles. For fear of the young man's life, she will psychologically train him to be mentally weak and dependent but physically strong. Because she has become psychologically independent, she will train her female offspring's to be psychologically independent. What have you got?*

*You've got the nigger woman out front and the man behind and scared. This is a perfect situation for sound sleep and economics. Before the breaking process, we had to alertly on guard at all times. Now we can sleep soundly, for out of frozen fear, his woman stands guard for us. He cannot get past her infant slave process. HE IS A GOOD TOOL, NOW READY TO BE TIED TO THE HORSE AT A TENDER AGE. By the time a nigger boy reaches the age of sixteen, he is soundly broken in and ready for life's sound and efficient work and the reproduction of a unit of good labour force.*

I believe Mr Lynch was under inspiration from the devil himself when he came up with this strategy. It is a despicable plan but, one thing we all have to agree on is that it works. It is a classic case of how experiences shape our perception and how they can teach us the wrong things – which we come to accept as the norm and live according to them.

The man is beaten to a pulp and humiliated in front of his wife, children and colleagues for a purpose. First of all, to make the woman realise that she cannot trust in the protection of the man. Naturally, she is inclined to trust that the man, as the family head and as the stronger vessel has to protect her and the children. Well, this humiliation proves her wrong. She realises there are other 'superior' men who she should be afraid of and from whom her husband cannot protect her. The man becomes a ceremonial head but true belief in him is gone. He will still be respected in his house but when the going gets tough, the woman would rather rely on the slave owner's protection than her man's.

There are many Christians who religiously attend church services and try as much as possible to lead holy lives. I mean, in many aspects of being Christian, they excel well but, when it comes to certain things like financial provision, they turn to worldly ways of getting money. Sometimes it is because they think God is not able to provide for them. Some are like that when it comes to health. They can quote and recite bible verses but when they are afflicted in their flesh, they may turn to witch doctors or any other thing besides God. They may give God a 'shot' by saying few words of prayer and maybe calling the local pastor but, deep in their hearts, they would believe in medicine more than God – the creator of it all. Many times if you dig deeper you realise it is probably because they have seen many people dying when 'they had believed in God'. Some of these people will tell you that God heals but heals if He wants. They may not necessarily doubt God's ability to heal but will always doubt if He will heal them or their loved ones.

This is NOT because has been beat by the devil before but because of the illusion that He was. It is this illusion that God will not help that the devil wants you to believe and have stuck in your head. You can say, but what else is there to believe if I once prayed and I wasn't healed? Or that you once prayed for someone and they did not get healed. That's exactly the confusion that the devil operates on. It results in many

Christians believing that the promises of God are theoretical and not practical.

Now there is a lot that happens with God's way of working on earth. The one essential thing is that everything about God works by faith. And then when it comes to the prayer of petition, factors like wisdom come into play as well.

*[Mathew 13:58] And He did not do many miracles there because of their unbelief. NASB*

The Lord Jesus, even though He was willing to perform miracles and heal the sick, He did not because of their unbelief. Some may say, but I believed in God when I asked for something that I did not get. It may be true but, most times we mistake presumption for faith and we also sometimes mistake our deep need for something for faith in the giver – God. And sometimes it is because we ask amiss – asking for things that are not in the specific Will of God for the time. The Lord Jesus was mocked by the Roman soldiers [Matthew 27:42] when they were saying "He saved others; He cannot save Himself. He is the King of Israel; let Him now come down from the cross, and we will believe in Him." The Lord Jesus has a well-documented history of miracles – including raising the dead. In-fact, he once disappeared in their faces [Luke 4:30] but, He had to go through crucifixion. He even told Peter that He had the power to fight the whole Roman empire but He had to live in the Specific Will of the Father.

*[Mathew 26:53] "Or do you think that I cannot appeal to My Father, and He will at once put at My disposal more than twelve legions of angels? "How then will the Scriptures be fulfilled, which say that it must happen this way?*

For lack of better words, there is what I can call the General Will of God and the Specific Will of God. There is what God has said, what God is saying and what God will say. The General Will of God is more about what God has already said. And what God has already said is in the Word of God. Every Christian needs to start there and understand what He has already said about everything. God wants us well and in perfect health.

The broken Christian will teach their child the same thing. And teaching is not all about having your kids sit down and you give them a lecture. The kids will always learn more from how you react in a crisis or a situation. Your children will learn to resort to spirit mediums if that is what you do when they are sick. Your children will also learn to be timid if that's your reaction to every confrontation. They know who you call when in a crisis and no matter what you say in their faces, what you do is what they will do.

v) <u>Culture</u>

One other powerful and decisive source of information is culture. Culture is a very difficult thing to deal with because some of what a person would think is a Christian belief is a cultural belief in essence. Cultural norms and beliefs are deeply ingrained in everyone and they come to the fore many times when we hard-pressed. The thing with a real belief is that it is what comes to the fore when we are in difficult situations. We may have ideas and concepts in our minds and our intellect can toy around with possibilities and concepts but, in a situation of real distress, what comes to the fore is the real belief.

I grew up believing that God will only help those who help themselves. I only realised that there was no scripture like that when I was an adult. It was spoken of frequently in Christian circles and I'm sure some people even quoted that statement behind pulpits and it just sounded right. It became a part of the cultural lenses through which I viewed the whole world. Do you know what this did to me? Each time I would try to 'help' God in some way. Whenever I had to ask God for anything in my life, I would end up trying to 'help' Him in a way because He would only someone who was also trying. I am in no way encouraging people to sit and not take charge of their situations but, I'm saying just like in [Matthew 6:25-34], the Lord Jesus instructs to be carefree. He instructs us to completely trust in Him and not worry about a thing.

But it is a hard thing to do, especially if you have grown up in such a culture to unlearn all that and completely put your trust in Him.

Affliction
In this called war, there are situations where these clashes are physical. Not that they become fights against flesh and blood but, the battle is felt and

experienced physically. It is through affliction. The Lord
Jesus says this about that subject:

*[Mathew 12:22 – 29] Then a demon-possessed man who
was blind and mute was brought to Jesus, and He
healed him, so that the mute man spoke and saw. All
the crowds were amazed, and were saying, "This man
cannot be the Son of David, can he?" But when the
Pharisees heard this, they said, "This man casts out
demons only by Beelzebul the ruler of the demons."
And knowing their thoughts Jesus said to them, "Any
kingdom divided against itself is laid waste; and any
city or house divided against itself will not stand. "If
Satan casts out Satan, he is divided against himself;
how then will his kingdom stand? "If I by Beelzebul cast
out demons, by whom do your sons cast them out? For
this reason they will be your judges. "But if I cast out
demons by the Spirit of God, then the kingdom of God
has come upon you. "Or how can anyone enter the
strong man's house and carry off his property, unless
he first binds the strong man? And then he will plunder
his house. NASB*

The Lord Jesus had just delivered a demon-possessed
man from a demon when he encountered the Pharisees.
They claimed that He was casting demons out by
Beelzebul, the ruler of the demons. He trashes their
argument using simple logic – no kingdom can be
divided against itself.

On top of mentioning that the devil has a kingdom, the
Lord Jesus makes a remarkable statement. He says "But
if I cast demons by the Spirit of God then the kingdom

of God has come upon you". He mentions the one time we see a direct clash between the Kingdom of God and the kingdom of the devil.

Let me say that I am about to venture into unpopular territory here. It has taken me some time to finally write about this. And I finally made this decision because I believe it will help some people out there. Recently I have come across many Christian churches that do not believe in the reality of demons in the church.

Remember the truth that we established in the previous chapters that when a man is born again, it is the spirit of man that is born again and is reconnected to God the father. And it is in the spirit of man that the Holy Spirit dwells. The corrupt soul of a man can be influenced by demons. I believe that a born-again Christian cannot be possessed by demons but that a Christian can be demonized. The Holy Spirit of God owns the Christian's spirit when he is born again but elements of a man's soul (corrupt from birth) can be controlled by demons.

I like how Pastor Vlad Savchuk puts it. I will paraphrase He says positionally, Christ gives you total victory over demons and sin but, you still have to go and fight. Not for victory but from victory. In my personal experience, I have seen and prayed for born-again Christians that were under demonic oppression and they were delivered. It is generally believed by many people that such people were never Christians in the first place. I think it is easy to make such statements coming from the seminary because they are theologically correct but, practically, the salvation of the soul of man is a progressive process. The spirit is saved, the soul is being saved and the body will be saved.

Demons can cause a lot of things in a person. Chief among them is sicknesses [Luke 13-10-16], [Matt 17:15-18]. Demons can also be responsible for blindness, deafness and being dumb [Matt 12:22]. These afflictions of the body can indeed drive man away from God, which is the devil's aim (We see this clearly in the affliction of Job) and sometimes are to make the demonized person ineffective in their ministry or their life. In some cases, such cases even lead to death.

*[Job 1:10 – 11] The Lord said to Satan, "Have you considered My servant Job? For there is no one like him on the earth, a blameless and upright man, fearing God and turning away from evil." Then Satan answered the Lord, "Does Job fear God for nothing? Have You not made a hedge about him and his house and all that he has, on every side? You have blessed the work of his hands, and his possessions have increased in the land. But put forth Your hand now and touch all that he has; he will surely curse You to Your face." NASB*

From this conversation between God and the devil, it is easy to pick that the devil thought that Job only worshipped and served God faithfully because of the blessings of God. He wanted to prove God wrong. The sole reason for afflicting Job was to get at God. The devil was waiting to say to God "I told you so." He thought by afflicting Job, he would turn against God and curse Him. Later events prove otherwise. Job loved and worshipped God unconditionally.

It is the same even today. One of the many reasons why the devil afflicts people is to draw them away from God. To turn humanity against God and sometimes the reason is to make people ineffective or to affects the different facets of their lives. It has always been his agenda. The other reason I believe is for the devil to propagate and orchestrate evil via the human faculties of the soul – that is to influence more people away from God. [1 Timothy 4:1-3] speaks of seducing spirits and doctrines of devils. The devil can seduce others into sin or propagate his doctrines through demonized people.

Demons also enslave people. They can keep people under the bondage of sin. Addictions are a clear example of this. A born-again Christian can be under the bondage of addictions – gambling, pornography or masturbation. Most times addictions do not go just because you tell yourself that you want to break the addiction. You may read many self-help books and make promises to yourself but, you will still find yourself relapsing. It is only the power of God that can completely set you free from addictions and most times, there are spirits behind all this. This may not be common in some cultures but there are what are called spiritual wives or spiritual husbands that some demonized people are joined to.

We must understand that demonization does not happen from the blue. You do not just wake up and you are demonized. Just like faith is what God uses with Christians, demonization also has its doors.

- Unforgiveness

The Lord Jesus instructed us to forgive offenders just like God forgives our sins. It is because God wants us to mirror His nature of love but, also to protect us from the possible effects of not forgiving. People go through a lot of things in their lives including abuse and hurt. Sexual abuse and rejection are major examples. If these experiences result in grief, bitterness or Unforgiveness, they open up doors to demons.

In their later years, victims can become perpetrators or develop other strange lusts. Many have been known to become homosexuals, prostitutes, molesters, domestic violence perpetrators etc.

Christians need to forgive even when it hurts. I know this is easier said than done but, with the help of the Lord, it is certainly possible. Christian parents must monitor make sure they love their children and raise them well in godly environments. It is critical because the future of their children rests on it.

- The occult

Any involvement in the occult is a direct invitation of demons of the occult into the life of an individual. The occult includes all forms of magic, witchcraft, New Age, Scientology, seeking spirit mediums and freemasonry. The list I have given is not exhaustive. There are many forms of the occult that people can be involved in that open doors to demons into the soul of a person.

One important thing to note is that it doesn't necessarily need a person to be directly involved in the occult to be affected by demons. Many indirect ways of involvement can cause demonization.

Family

One family member can open the doorway to demons in a family by their involvement in the occult. Knowing our ancestry is very important and can help us discover a lot. In my African culture, it was normal for family heads to get involved in the occult to protect the family. It was treated as a noble thing but, it has resulted in a lot of suffering and demonization in the lives of the newer generations. Some people were dedicated to demons as part of the demonic covenants that were entered into.

In my Shona culture, we know of people that were given to fighting spirits. These people grow up to be extremely violent people with unmatched demonic strength when it comes to fighting.

When my father married my mother, he was given charms to protect him and my mother was also given objects that were meant to protect her. When they found Christ, they both agreed to denounce that occult involvement and they burnt the objects and prayed. Hallelujah.

Relationships

Relationships create what are called soul ties and these soul ties can be gateways to demons. There are a lot of people that have been initiated in the occult because of sexual encounters with people involved in the occult. It is also important to note that it may not be a person's partner who is directly involved in the occult but maybe their family members.

All I'm trying to say is that demonization doesn't happen to people in psychiatric wards or solitary confinement. The people you meet every day on your way to work can have demons oppressing them.

Accursed Objects

Supernatural power flows in this realm through objects – people and even material objects. [Acts 19:11-12]. Demonic power also can flow through objects and places. There are anointed people, anointed places and anointed objects. In the same manner, there are accursed places, people and objects. Unsuspecting believers can get possession of accursed objects and bring demons into their lives because of this. In my culture, it was very common for people to receive objects (of any form – including cloths or clay pots) that were meant to protect them. These objects were accursed and would bring demons into the lives of the protected

It is the same thing with accursed places. We know of haunted houses from movies and we also know of graveyards as the common scene for magical rituals. It's not just a Hollywood idea, it is based on what happens in real life. Of course, you will go to the cemetery to bury your dead but, believers should not be unnecessarily be involved with places like shrines which are dedicated to devils. Whenever we go to the cemetery with my family, my father always prays to state our right to visit the cemetery in remembrance of our loved ones and denouncing any involvement with the occult.

Whenever we would move to a new house, my parents would pray over the new property, pleading the blood of Jesus over it and denouncing any sin or occult activity that could have happened on the property before our occupation. Thank God, I learnt a lot from them.

Travellers, it is good to collect souvenirs but, make sure you don't end up with accursed objects from the occult. Parents, try to have control over what your children bring to the house. The posters they have in their bedrooms, the friends they associate with and where they go.

- Sin:

Sin is an open door to demonization. By continuous committing of sin, a person enters into a covenant of character with the world of evil and this opens doors to demonic forces that promote that sin. It becomes increasingly difficult to conquer that sin because it ceases to be just an act the person decides to engage in but becomes an expression of the demon oppressing the person.

Anyone who has had to fight any addiction of any sort will understand this. The trap that many people are in is thinking that they can stop any habit whenever they want. Someone addicted to pornography and/or masturbation may believe they can stop it when they want. They only find out that they cannot the day they decide to. And the more one tries to free stop by themselves the more they keep going back. It is only the name of the Lord that delivered [Joel 2:32]

The Bible asks us not to give a foothold to the devil. [Eph 4:27]

Decision Making
The first operational tactic (building strongholds) is a long term strategy and is the grand scheme in the war but the battle that every individual will fight every day is the decision-making battle and each decision is influenced by the strongholds.

Because we are free moral agents, we chart our courses by the decisions we make daily. The blueprint for tomorrow is today. That is it. And as you can easily conclude, it goes beyond what one individual does from the day they are born. Yes, that is essential but the environment they find themselves in is largely determined by the decisions made by their predecessors.

Therefore, decision making has ripple effects. A decision made by a parent today will have a significant impact on the life of a child years to come and the life of a grandchild a generation later. Where we are, as individuals, in life is largely dependent on the choices we made and the choices made by other people that affect us indirectly or directly.

Because a decision has such power, the devil makes it a priority to wage war on this front. He tries in all ways possible to influence our decisions, hence our lives. In essence, the whole point of temptation is to sway decisions made by the one tempted.

Priming

There is a concept in psychology called priming which refers to a process of accessing schemas a person holds in their mind. Schemas on a basic level are a set of facts, stereotypes or beliefs one holds pertaining a subject or an entity. Thus, a person can have a lot of different schemas about the different things in life. Schemas are no different from strongholds. Like we established already, strongholds are beliefs.

When one makes a judgement, they refer to schemas they hold and make a judgement using the most accessible schema. A practical example is this, if you see a man beating up his wife in public, you can make a judgement about that person depending on the most accessible schema you hold. You can use your schema about men in general to make a judgement. If you hold it in your schema that men are abusive by nature then you will probably assume that the act is a result of that. At the same time, you may have a schema about women that holds the belief that women are provocative by nature. Using this schema you can assume that the woman has provoked the man into the beating. One act can be explained by different schemas and the schema that one uses at any instance is largely dependent on the most available schema. This is the schema that is at the forefront of our minds. Priming now is a process of accessing the schemas that one has. It is a process of bringing schemas to the forefront of our minds to influence a decision to be made using the schema brought to the forefront.

In an interrogation, a detective may try to get information out of a suspect by bringing to the forefront, the schema they hold about jail. In the end, the suspect, though holding a schema about friendship (which may prohibit him from disclosing accomplices), may end up ratting out accomplices because of the schema of jail that is brought to the forefront of his mind to the forefront during the interrogation process.

In psychology, there are subliminal and supraliminal methods of priming. Subliminal priming is below the level of consciousness. This happens when a person is not even aware that they are being primed. Supraliminal priming occurs at a consciously perceivable level.

Remember that we established that man, in his old nature, is corrupt therefore, the schemas he holds in his soul about everything are corrupt and earthbound. The born-again Christian also may have strongholds (schemas) in their minds that are corrupt and based on lies, heresy or inaccurate scripture interpretation. On the other hand, the born again spirit of man receives schemas based on the truth of the word of God that may be contrary to the schemas held in the soul of a man.

What then happens to a person daily is making decisions on any step or action. The question is, which schema will a person use in any circumstance. Will they use the corrupt schema of the flesh or the spiritual schema inspired by the truth of the word of God? This is the heart of spiritual warfare ladies and gentlemen. When a beautiful lady throws herself at the feet of a married Christian brother, is he going to go with the integrity schema or is he going to go with the 'grace' schema? If he has been taught liberal grace he may go with that? But shall we continue sinning because grace abounds? God forbid. I must state that, in reality, there is nothing like too much grace; there are just people that take advantage of it.

When faced with sickness, will a born again Christian lady call the family witch doctor or will she depend on the Lord? When pulled over by the police for over speeding will a pastor pay the fine or give a bribe? This is the heart of spiritual warfare brethren.

I am from a country where it is almost impossible to get a driver's licence without paying a bribe. Will one retreat behind the statement 'it is what it is' or they will go for multiple tests and fail because they did not bribe.

In any case, the Christian is supposed to spend time in the word of God and prayer. This is priming. This makes the schemas from your spirit more accessible to your mind. They stay at the forefront of your mind that in any case, you make the right decisions and you overcome the flesh. When the Apostle Paul speaks of setting our minds on things above, this is what He means.

*[Colossians 3:1-4] Therefore if you have been raised up with Christ, keep seeking the things above, where Christ is, seated at the right hand of God. Set your mind on the things above, not on the things that are on earth. For you have died and your life is hidden with Christ in God. When Christ, who is our life, is revealed, then you also will be revealed with Him in glory. NASB*

If you spend your time watching porn and reading explicit novels you are likely to pick the 'for all have fallen short' verse instead of 'we are dead to sin' one when the day of temptation comes.

Temptation
*[James 1:14 -15] But each one is tempted when he is carried away and enticed by his own lust. Then when lust has conceived, it gives birth to sin; and when sin is accomplished, it brings forth death. NASB*

Temptation works on the same grounds. Each man has desires and lusts and these are what tempt us. The devil and demons have been around for a long time that they know the basic desires of man. The devil, via agents (demons), studies each individual to the point that they can easily anticipate your reaction to a certain circumstance. I mean, if Google can anticipate videos you may like, the devil knows even your type. It is on this information that he presents enticements to you.

A classic case is that of our Lord Jesus in the wilderness:

*[Matthew 4"1-11] Then Jesus was led up by the Spirit into the wilderness to be tempted by the devil. And after He had fasted forty days and forty nights, He then became hungry.[3] And the tempter came and said to Him, "If You are the Son of God, command that these stones become bread."[4] But He answered and said, "It is written, 'Man shall not live on bread alone, but on every word that proceeds out of the mouth of God.'"[5] Then the devil *took Him into the holy city and had Him stand on the pinnacle of the temple,[6] and *said to Him, "If You are the Son of God, throw Yourself down; for it is written, 'He will command His angels concerning You'; and 'On their hands they will bear You up,*

*So that You will not strike Your foot against a stone.'"[7] Jesus said to him, "On the other hand, it is written, 'You shall not put the Lord your God to the test.'"[8] Again, the devil *took Him to a very high* *mountain and *showed Him all the kingdoms of the world and their glory;[9] and he said to Him, "All these things I will give You, if You fall down and worship me."[10] Then Jesus *said to him, "Go, Satan! For it is written, 'You shall worship the Lord your God, and serve Him only.'"[11] Then the devil *left Him; and behold, angels came and began to minister to Him. NASB*

In the first two instances, the devil is priming a certain schema. The devil knows Jesus is the Son of God and he knows what it entails to be a Son of God. The devil knows a Son of God has power and is trying to bring this to the forefront of Jesus' mind so that He makes a decision basing on this. But because Jesus had been praying and fasting for forty days and nights, He rightly knows which attribute or fact of being a Son of God has to work in the situation. And that attribute is obedience to the Will of God and not His own.

In the third instance, the devil tries to appeal to the desire in all men of good living, power and glory. He then attaches a price to it, which is worship.

It is important to note that much of our failures are due to trying to pursue good things in the wrong way or by wrong methods. Jesus has power over all the kingdom of the devil [Eph 1:20-21] because He chose to go it the hard way. Many times the easy way out of a situation is a trap. There is a process with everything. And you have to be willing to go through it. For as long as the earth remains, there shall be seedtime and harvest. [Gen 8:22].

Never try to reap where you did not sow. That is one of the traps in life. And, patience is a virtue. There is a saying that 'good things come to those who wait' and I find it to be right on the money. My generation is used to instant fact-checking, instant messaging etc. All good things but, this has led many to believe that everything in life has to be quick like that. It takes time to have and build anything that truly lasts. It is a principle and it can save you from the dangers of shortcuts in life.

Always remember this whenever you have to make a career decision or even a marriage decision. Never sacrifice principle on the altar of expediency.


The devil has been deceiving people over the four cardinal questions of life- origin, morality, purpose and destiny. Even when the devil afflicts, he is trying to get you away from your dependence on God. He wants you to believe it is God who brings affliction on mankind.

# Chapter Eight

The Kingdom of God

It would do little justice to talk about the kingdom of darkness and not talk about the kingdom of God. Many believers do not have a hard time understanding the Kingdom of God because it is one of the most widely taught subjects. However, we have to establish some truths about it in this chapter so that we can better understand how we should wage war.

The kingdom of God is almost all that Jesus taught about. His sole mandate was to bring back the kingdom of God. From the previous chapters, we have established that man, through Adam's sin declared his independence from God. Jesus, the last Adam [1 Cor 15:45] came back to restore that relationship with God the Father. We understand generally that a kingdom is a domain in which a king exercises His dominion. God is the king and we, the believers, are the subjects.

After God created the earth in the book of Genesis, we established that He appointed man as His vice-regent on earth. He gave man dominion over the earth [Gen 1:26]. Through the fall, man lost connection to God. Here is how I understand the concept of kingdoms and satellite states/colonies. Zimbabwe, where I come from, was once colonised by the British government. At the time it was called Southern Rhodesia (from around 1923 to 1965). Colonies' administration was run by the metropolitan states (the mother countries) and that was the case with Zimbabwe and Britain. It was only in 1965 that Ian Smith declared independence from Britain in what was known as the Unilateral Declaration of Independence and Southern Rhodesia came to be known as Rhodesia, an unrecognized state that existed from 1965 to 1979. It wasn't officially recognised because it declared Independence from the Mother country. This was followed by economic sanctions imposed on Rhodesia – trade with the former colony was banned etc. This was an attempt to make the Smith government give in.

I am in no way comparing God to the British government but, this concept will allow us to understand what happened to man in the garden of Eden. The fall was man's declaration of independence from God and as such, man lived on earth in separation from God. Man's spirit was disconnected from the source of all power and life. Jesus comes back as the life-giving Spirit, as we mentioned in the previous chapters, through regeneration and restores this relationship between God and man.

This is why He was always preaching about the Kingdom of God. Before the coming of Jesus, the devil took advantage and terrorised man on earth and fought hard to prevent the plan of God to restore the relationship. Herod tried hard to kill all male children because He knew that God had a plan to redeem humanity through the seed of a woman mentioned in [Genesis 3].

*[Mathew 4:17] From that time Jesus began to preach and say, "Repent, for the kingdom of heaven is at hand." NASB*

After regeneration, a Christian is restored in the kingdom of God and is in fellowship with God again. The Kingdom of God, in as much as access to it, is gained on a personal level, it is a kingdom with a timetable (The Will of God), a code of conduct (the leadership by the Holy Spirit) and a hierarchy. The hierarchy is what most people fail to understand and observe. No-one doubts the supreme authority of God and the headship of Jesus over the church. It is the issue of ranks from there that has people confused. This also is unpopular territory. Let us look at the verse that we discussed on in the previous chapters.

*[Daniel 10:13] "But the prince of the kingdom of Persia was withstanding me for twenty-one days; then behold, Michael, one of the chief princes, came to help me, for I had been left there with the kings of Persia. NASB*

The verse outlines an issue about rank in the kingdom of heaven (the one which we mirror on earth as the church). The angel Gabriel (a messenger) was fought by a demonic prince and was withstood for 21 days until another high ranking angel (Michael) had to come and help. Remember when we established that in the kingdom of satan there are ranks. There are high ranking princes then rulers over areas and subareas and then the foot soldiers. It is the same in the Kingdom of God.

It is not just an issue of being born again and you say that's it. YES, that is it but, there is more. YES if you die you will go to heaven because, after all, that is what makes us go to heaven but, if you want to live fully in the Kingdom, there is structure and other principles that have to be observed. The principle of honour is chief among them.

We have to understand another dimension of authority as Christians. There is primary authority and then there is delegated authority. The source of primary authority is God Himself. He is the omnipotent God who created all things. He, therefore, has the right to command and we must obey. Then there is delegated authority – authority given to other parties by a party with primary authority.

God's primary authority was delegated to Jesus. The Lord Jesus was the perfect image of God Himself and was acknowledged by God. [Mathew 3:17]

*[Mathew 28:18] And Jesus came up and spoke to them, saying, "All authority has been given to Me in heaven and on earth. NASB*

Then this authority was delegated to the Apostles.

*"Sanctify them in the truth; Your word is truth. "As You sent Me into the world, I also have sent them into the world. NASB*

The apostles were given authority to teach and instruct the church and exercised the authority. The Apostles also wrote authoritatively to the church. It is from their letters and books that we learn of kingdom principles and how to lead. These apostles also wrote about delegated authorities that we have to honour and fall under.

Parental authority

The immediate authority that everyone has to submit to is parental authority. God primarily demands us to obey our parents to teach us obedience to Him. This is clearly stated in several scriptures.

[Ephesians 6: 1 – 4] *Children, obey your parents in the Lord, for this is right. HONOR YOUR FATHER AND MOTHER (which is the first commandment with a promise), SO THAT IT MAY BE WELL WITH YOU, AND THAT YOU MAY LIVE LONG ON THE EARTH. Fathers, do not provoke your children to anger, but bring them up in the discipline and instruction of the Lord. NASB*

Including [Col 3:20] these verses explicitly tell children to obey their parents. Now, there is a spirit of rebellion that operates in teenagers and young people that tries to lure them into the trap of disobedience. The Apostle mentioned that it was the first commandment with a promise. A promise of doing well in life and having a long life. This is a potential trap for Christians who have parents that are not saved. The temptation is to disrespect them because they do not know God but the bible does not instruct us to obey only Christian parents.

I am convinced that many premature deaths and some hardships in life are a result of disobedience to parents. God is a God of order and principle. You will waste away your time and energy fasting and praying for a long life and grace to make it in life. It is clear right there in the Bible. Obey your parents and you will live long and succeed in life. The devil will have you suspecting bewitchment or bad luck when some of the problems are brought on us because we dishonour delegated authority.

Before you set out to fight demons of limitations and near misses, start examining your relationship with your parents. If you have dishonoured them, humble yourself and go back to them and apologize. Make amends and maintain a respectful relationship with them.

*[Heb. 12:5-6] "... My son, regard not lightly the chastening of the Lord, nor faint when thou art reproved of him: for whom the Lord loveth he chasteneth and scourgeth every son whom he receiveth."KJV*

Ecclesiastical Authority
*For this reason I left you in Crete, that you would set in order what remains and appoint elders in every city as I directed you, 6 namely, if any man is above reproach, the husband of one wife, having children who believe, not accused of dissipation or rebellion. For the [a]overseer must be above reproach as God's steward, not self-willed, not quick-tempered, not addicted to wine, not pugnacious, not fond of sordid gain, but hospitable, loving what is good, sensible, just, devout,*

*self-controlled, holding fast the faithful word which is in accordance with the teaching, so that he will be able both to exhort in sound doctrine and to refute those who contradict.*

*For there are many rebellious men, empty talkers and deceivers, especially those of the circumcision, who must be silenced because they are upsetting whole families, teaching things they should not teach for the sake of sordid gain. One of themselves, a prophet of their own, said, "Cretans are always liars, evil beasts, lazy gluttons." This testimony is true. For this reason reprove them severely so that they may be sound in the faith, not paying attention to Jewish myths and commandments of men who turn away from the truth. To the pure, all things are pure; but to those who are defiled and unbelieving, nothing is pure, but both their mind and their conscience are defiled. They profess to know God, but by their deeds they deny Him, being detestable and disobedient and worthless for any good deed. NASB*

Titus was instructed to appoint elders over cities who other believers had to submit to. They were also supposed to be available to teach sound doctrine. Some rebellious men were taking it upon themselves to teach when they were not qualified to do so. The Kingdom of God is a kingdom of order and hierarchy that must be honoured. Some qualities were expected from elders. They had to meet certain criteria.

This is not legalism. It just goes to show that in as much as we will all go to heaven, within the kingdom, some roles and responsibilities cannot be assumed by everyone. It is based on principle. Do you remember from the kingdom of darkness some evil rulers are responsible for peddling strongholds and heresies? In the kingdom of God, there are also authorities responsible for teaching the true doctrine of Christ. It is not everyone. So in this spiritual warfare, one has to understand their role and their duties. A foot soldier is not to be found in planning attacks.

In every man's soul, there is an inclination to rebellion. The old nature of man has rebellious tendencies and has to be brought to the obedience of Christ daily. God gives grace to the humble and resists the proud.

The elders are also given the grace to pray for the sick so that they recover

*[James 5:14-16] Is any sick among you? let him call for the elders of the church; and let them pray over him, anointing him with oil in the name of the Lord: KJV*

This does not mean that God will not heal you if you pray for yourself. We have to understand that the authority of God flows through delegated authorities. Some battles need a higher authority. Some problems need a higher ecclesiastical authority to be dealt with.

The tenth chapter of the book of Acts narrates an interesting story. There was a devout man named Cornelius who gave alms, feared the Lord with all His household and also prayed continually to God. One day God shows him a vision and in the vision, he was instructed to send for the Apostle Peter. The Lord's answer to Cornelius prayers was an Apostle. When the Apostle Peter went to Cornelius' house, he did not even need to pray. His presence and testimony led to the whole household receiving the Holy Spirit and they all began speaking in tongues.

Civil Authority

The Christian finds himself in a family, then in a church and then under civil authority. From the local authorities to the government. Scripture instructs us to respect this authority unless obedience to civil authority means disobeying God.

*[Romans 13:1-7] Everyone must submit to governing authorities. For all authority comes from God, and those in positions of authority have been placed there by God. [2] So anyone who rebels against authority is rebelling against what God has instituted, and they will be punished. [3] For the authorities do not strike fear in people who are doing right, but in those who are doing wrong. Would you like to live without fear of the authorities? Do what is right, and they will honor you. [4] The authorities are God's servants, sent for your good. But if you are doing wrong, of course you should be afraid, for they have the power to punish you. They are God's servants, sent for the very purpose of punishing those who do what is wrong. [5] So you must submit to them, not only to avoid punishment, but also to keep a clear conscience. Pay your taxes, too, for these same reasons. For government workers need to be paid. They are serving God in what they do. [7] Give to*

*everyone what you owe them: Pay your taxes and government fees to those who collect them, and give respect and honor to those who are in authority. NLT*

The ideal situation is having a godly government, then having a local church leader submitting to God and finally parents that fear the Lord. That way, you know that the chain of command comes flows smoothly to you as a believer. But, this is not always the case. We have since established that the prince of Tyre and the king of Babylon were rulers that were under the influence of the devil.

This was the same scenario in the times of the Persian Empire, the Greeks and then the Romans. [Daniel 2]. The powerful kingdoms to exist on earth were under the influence of the devil and they came in direct contrast with the will of God. The Church suffered serious persecution at the hands of these rulers. In fact, of all the Lord's disciples, only the Apostle John is believed to have died a natural death. All the other Apostles were persecuted and killed. This is usually the case in the world we live in. We find ourselves under governments that are looking after the legalities of every citizen. This being a fundamental attribute of democracy, the drawback for Christians is that democracy also has to accommodate the rights of homosexuals and other false religions.

Some governments in the Middle East are actually against the Bible. In these circumstances, the stance to take is not obedience. Sometimes it is not wise to just disobey too. What has to be understood by the church is that in Babylon, Daniel, Shadrach, Misheck and Abednego were persecuted after they refused to obey the king's orders but, it wasn't only disobedience. Daniel rose to prominence in the nation of Babylon and changed the stance towards believers. Daniel mastered the gift that the Lord had given him and his gift brought him before the king.

We as the church should be raising people that can rise and take up influential positions in the world systems we find ourselves in. Yes, the church can pray and fast against the promotion of sin in a land but, the war can be easier and more permanently won by raising people that can take up decision making positions in the local councils up to the governments. It will be a lot easier for a Christian President to simply ban homosexuality than it is for the church to pray against it. Strategy is important for the Church to understand.


The Christian's responsibility
The Christian, in the light of all the truths we have established then has to take a stance. The general mandate of every Christian was given by the Lord Jesus Himself in the Great Commission.

*[Matthew 28:16-20]* [16] *But the eleven disciples proceeded to Galilee, to the mountain which Jesus had designated.* [17] *When they saw Him, they worshiped Him; but some were doubtful.* [18] *And Jesus came up and spoke to them, saying, "All authority has been given to Me in heaven and on earth.* [19] *Go therefore and make*

*disciples of all the nations, baptizing them in the name of the Father and the Son and the Holy Spirit, <sup>20</sup> teaching them to observe all that I commanded you; and lo, I am with you always, even to the end of the age." NASB*

This is the great commission. Every believer is mandated to go into the world with the good news of Christ. The good news of the Kingdom of God. Whether you find yourself affiliated to a local church or not, the primary goal of the kingdom is making disciples of Christ. Advancing the kingdom of God is God's heart and can be achieved in many different ways. Our Lord Jesus Christ has given gifts to some to be Apostles, some to be Prophets, some to be Pastors, some to be teachers and some to be evangelists. These are commonly known as the five-fold ministry.

The five-fold Ministry
The book will not dwell much on this subject but, I will highlight the importance. Some Christians have been called into what is called the five-fold ministry. These are offices that are responsible for specialised advancement of the kingdom of God and the perfecting of the saints – the church.

*[Ephesians 4:11-12] And he gave some, apostles; and some, prophets; and some, evangelists; and some, pastors and teachers;*

*<sup>12</sup> For the perfecting of the saints, for the work of the ministry, for the edifying of the body of Christ:*

It is not everyone who is called into these offices but some are. Those who are called have to wage war from these offices and understand their roles and responsibilities.

# Chapter Nine

Walking in Victory

What has to be understood by every believer is that we are not fighting for victory but, we are fighting from victory. The enemy we face is a defeated foe. The Bible speaks of him as like a roaring lion, seeking whom to devour, but he isn't a lion at all. It was on the cross that the Lord Jesus disarmed him completely.

*[Colossians 2:8 - 19] Therefore as you have received Christ Jesus the Lord, <u>so walk in Him</u>, having been firmly rooted and now being built up in Him and established in your faith, just as you were instructed, and overflowing with gratitude. <u>See to it that no one takes you captive through philosophy and empty deception, according to the tradition of men, according to the elementary principles of the world</u>, rather than according to Christ. For in Him all the fullness of Deity dwells in bodily form, and <u>in Him you have been made complete</u>, and <u>He is the head over all rule and authority;</u> and in Him you were also circumcised with a circumcision made without hands, in the removal of the body of the flesh by the circumcision of Christ; having been buried with Him in baptism, in which you were also raised up with Him through faith in the working of God, who raised Him from the dead. When you were dead in your transgressions and the uncircumcision of your flesh<u>, He</u>*

_made you alive together with Him, having forgiven us all our transgressions, having canceled out the certificate of debt consisting of decrees against us, which was hostile to us; and He has taken it out of the way, having nailed it to the cross. When He had disarmed the rulers and authorities, He made a public display of them, having triumphed over them through Him._

_Therefore no one is to act as your judge in regard to food or drink or in respect to a festival or a new moon or a Sabbath day— things which are a mere shadow of what is to come; but the substance belongs to Christ. Let no one keep defrauding you of your prize by delighting in self-abasement and the worship of the angels, taking his stand on visions he has seen, inflated without cause by his fleshly mind, and not holding fast to the head, from whom the entire body, being supplied and held together by the joints and ligaments, grows with a growth which is from God. NASB_

The only thing required is to walk in the knowledge that the war was already won and fight from a position of victory, not for victory. The enemy we fight capitalises on ignorance and deception. Like Sun Tzu said, all warfare is based on deception. The Apostle Paul hammered this point home in his letter to the Colossians quoted above.

The first thing he instructs the church to do is to walk in Him (Christ).

i)   Walk in Christ. Clear your Mind

*[Matthew 6:31 - 34] Be not therefore anxious, saying, What shall we eat? or, What shall we drink? or, Wherewithal shall we be clothed? For after all these things do the Gentiles seek; for your heavenly Father knoweth that ye have need of all these things. But seek ye first his kingdom, and his righteousness; and all these things shall be added unto you. Be not therefore anxious for the morrow: for the morrow will be anxious for itself. Sufficient unto the day is the evil thereof. NASB*

Walking in Christ means shifting our attention from the worries of the world we live in and focusing on the things of the world we come from. It is important to clear our minds first before we look to play our roles in the family, local church and our society. When battleships are at sea in formation, each ship has to know how it has to manoeuvre to fulfil the battle plan. Each captain in a ship has to have a clear picture of the battle plan and where it fits in the battle plan. This is why we have been talking about the Kingdom of God and its mandate, its structures and how things work in it.

On top of that, for the ship itself to be able to manoeuvre at all, it must be in the right shape. If it is steam-powered, the engine must be in the right shape. The anchors have to be working as well as the rudder. This is the same as the Christian. The Christian has to know his mandate and place within the grand plan of expanding the kingdom of God and also be in the right state in their being to be able to fight the battle.

This is why it is imperative to win the battle within. It is critical to be stable from within. We have to achieve this by first realising and accepting the fact that we are aliens in this world and that we are completely new people from the moment we receive Christ. This is very important. Our spirits are born again are a completely new creature in the image and power of Christ Himself. We have to be led by this revelation.

We have to then undergo a process of transformation. From being controlled by our souls to being led by the Spirit of God. The Bible says *For as many as are led by the Spirit of God, they are the sons of God [Romans 8:14]*.

There has to be a cultural shift as well. Obsession over what to eat and what to wear has to become a thing of the past. Being a citizen of God means that God becomes our sole provider and He instructs us to stop worrying about provision. The focus has to be on the kingdom and His righteousness then all the other needs are taken of. In other words, make God's business yours and He will make yours His. Thus, the anxiety and worry that comes with being a citizen of the world have to be let go. The survival instincts that make us anxious and worried about tomorrow have to be laid off because the kingdom we become members of is eternal and is led by the owner of everything. [Psalms 24:1]

We have to be transformed by the renewing of our minds. And not conformed to the world.

## ii) Break Free from Deception

The second thing to do after realising that we are citizens of a superior Kingdom is to familiarise ourselves with the nature of the Kingdom. There is a constitution of the Kingdom of God and is the Bible. We have to read it and know it. This is the only way we can dispel deception and lies accumulated from the world. One can be incapacitated by philosophy or traditions of men. All these have to be thrown out of the window. Where the traditions of man say healing comes from sangomas, the kingdom says it is our bread. Where science came with ideas like evolution, we replace with the truth – Creation by an eternal and Omnipotent being. We fight strongholds and pull them down by the power of the Word of God. The weapons of our warfare are not carnal...but they are strong to the pulling down of strongholds. The amount of revelation one has about God is what determines how effectively he can operate in the Kingdom of God.

## iii) Understand Primary and Delegated Authority

One has to fully understand the capacity of the power we have in the kingdom of God – Unlimited. One also has to understand how authority is delegated in the kingdom. Not only authority but roles. The soldiers on a battleship have to understand where battle orders come from for the sake of order. Every well-run kingdom has structure and protocol that must be observed.

iv) Understand your relationships

The next thing would be to understand how everyone is related to the Kingdom. We are all children of God. That makes us brothers and sisters

One pertinent fact to always remember is that our relationship with the father is not based on anything but by love. He is a loving father who loved us even before we knew Him. [1 John 4:19 ] We are not trying to be in His kingdom by our works. We get into the kingdom because He draws us to Him [John 6:44] and living right is our response to His love and a result of His holy nature that we received when we got born again.

Therefore, do not let anyone be your judge with regards to keeping laws and commandments. This is not a passport to sin but it is the nature of grace.

The enemy thrives on deception. A lot of people have been silenced because of condemnation. It is a journey until our souls are in perfect alignment with the image of Christ. In that process, we may act out of the character of Christ but that does not take away our citizenship.

*[Romans 8:1-2] Therefore there is now no condemnation for those who are in Christ Jesus. [2] For the law of the Spirit of life in Christ Jesus has set you free from the law of sin and of death. NASB*

Fight

After understanding all this, the next thing to do is to fight. We have discovered the schemes of the devil as well as the grand plan. Knowing the enemy's plans is part of the battle won, having a plan to attack the enemy does even more. Now, there is ammunition and combat gear to fight with. Take up the armour of God and fight. From the circumference of our anchor text, we get to understand that there is an armour that we have to make use of.

*[Ephesians 6:10-20] Finally, be strong in the Lord and in his mighty power. [11] Put on the full armor of God, so that you can take your stand against the devil's schemes. [12] For our struggle is not against flesh and blood, but against the rulers, against the authorities, against the powers of this dark world and against the spiritual forces of evil in the heavenly realms. [13] Therefore put on the full armor of God, so that when the day of evil comes, you may be able to stand your ground, and after you have done everything, to stand. [14] Stand firm then, with the belt of truth buckled around your waist, with the breastplate of righteousness in place, [15] and with your feet fitted with the readiness that comes from the gospel of peace. [16] In addition to all this, take up the shield of faith, with which you can extinguish all the flaming arrows of the evil one. [17] Take the helmet of salvation and the sword of the Spirit, which is the word of God. [18] And pray in the Spirit on all occasions with all kinds of prayers and*

The apostle Paul mentions the need to put on the full armour. Not just parts of it. Realising victory is dependent on how well you prepare and stand your ground. We talked about the relationship we have with God. A relationship based on the righteousness of Christ Jesus and not our works [Romans 3:22]. Understanding and living in this righteousness is the breastplate for the believer. The devil is known as the accuser of the brethren [1 Timothy 4:13]. Sometimes it is our consciences that condemn us when we act out of character. But you do not have to let this incapacitate you.

Your judgement has to be corrected by the word of God and thus recalibrating your conscience. Remember from the imago Dei which we bear, our conscience is meant to be the judge of our actions against our beliefs. It can take a while to recalibrate your conscience but it has to be done. Move from the legalistic way of thinking.

Faith is the shield that we use to extinguish the fiery arrows of the devil. The Bible speaks of faith as the substance of things hoped for, the evidence on things not seen [Hebrews 11:1]. The devil will always attack and he attacks us via our flesh points. The devil will try to tempt us or to discourage us through our flesh (body and soul) but it is only faith that can keep us going. It is easy to believe what is seen but what is unseen is more real. We walk by faith and not by sight [2 Cor 5:7].

There will come times in everyone's life where every circumstance will seem to be spelling absolute doom. When life has your back against the wall and from a human perspective, it looks like the world is crumbling at your feet. It can come in any way or form. It can be sickness, it can be a financial crisis or anything. The goal of the devil in all these afflictions is to make you turn on God and lose your faith and trust in Him. But, remember, all these arrows are extinguished by an inexplicable knowledge in our hearts, a certainty. The knowledge that Christ conquered all principalities and we walk from a position of victory. There is a peace that surpasses all human understanding that will keep you smiling even amid all the attacks.

Being a Christian does not mean we will not go through trying times. It means that even when we go through the waters, we do not let the waters get into us. Even when the world is scared, we are not. Because remember, we walk by faith and not by said. We are not afraid because He who is us is greater than who is in the world.

The Christian has to understand what salvation is. What it is that Christ accomplished at the cross and how salvation relates to the whole being of man – spirit, soul and body. His spirit is saved, his soul is being saved and his body will be saved. This is likened to the helmet of salvation; a critical piece in the armour of God. The head is a critical organ and has to be protected in battle. Many have doubted their salvation because of the stark contrast between their regenerated spirits and their souls.

This is why the Christian has to renewing his mind every day. Right after receiving the Lord Jesus as his personal Lord and Saviour, the Christian will find himself with negative thoughts. He may still think of sin but this does not mean he hasn't been saved. It is doubt emanating from this that can be fatal to the Christian and the devil revels in this confusion. Stand tall, and keep on; a righteous man may fall many times but the Lord picks Him up. It is a process until all the times the Christian's mind is fully focused on things above.

The soul of the Christian included his emotions as well; These are not the basis of his salvation. They fluctuate. There are moments when the Christian will feel they are saved and then days when he will not feel it. It all doesn't matter. His relationship with God is spiritual and the spirit is constant. Regardless of how he feels, he remains a child of God and must move in that conviction. His mind may still entertain some concepts and ideas but his spirit is saved. It is this understanding that is very imperative and must be kept at all times.

Then the Apostle Paul mentions the weapon that is used to attack. The sword of the Spirit, which is the word of God; The Christian attacks with the word of God. Strongholds are destroyed by the word of God.

Things are spoken into existence by speaking the word of God. Health is declared based on the word of God. It is the word of God that expands the Kingdom.

Prayer is an essential part of spiritual warfare; thanksgiving, petition and supplication. Depending on his need, the Christian has to be praying at all times. He may not be asking for anything all the times but in all situations, thanksgiving can be made. Much has been written on the subject of prayer and praying in the Spirit. This book will not focus much on that.

Lastly, the Christian is instructed to keep praying for the advancement of the kingdom. This is not limited to his efforts but also includes praying for the efforts of fellow soldiers and the local church. It can span denominations. The war is waged by every believer, regardless of denomination. Therefore, the Christian has to keep praying for this.

# Chapter Ten

## Keep Walking

It is important to understand that the calling to be a Christian does not mean you fight full time and you do not have a life. The battle is fought everyday incessantly as people go about their business. Some dedicated soldiers can be strategizing and equipping the saints but every other Christian is not called to be operating in these offices.

It is important to understand that advancing the kingdom is done even in the marketplace. We preach the kingdom of God more by our conduct than by our words. In the book of Exodus 31:

*Then the Lord said to Moses, $^2$ "See, I have chosen Bezalel son of Uri, the son of Hur, of the tribe of Judah, $^3$ and I have filled him with the Spirit of God, with wisdom, with understanding, with knowledge and with all kinds of skills— $^4$ to make artistic designs for work in gold, silver and bronze, $^5$ to cut and set stones, to work in wood, and to engage in all kinds of crafts. NIV*

The Lord anointed Bezalel and Oholiab with excellence in crafts. The gifts of God are not limited to the four corners of the church. Remember that the initial plan of God was for man to dominate the earth and represent God here. It is still His Will that every one of us rises and dominates in their pillar of society. The leaders should lead, entertainers must entertain. Everyone has to master their craft. This is how we conquer the earth.

From the rising of the sun each morning to its setting every evening, men and women toil. Children also wake up in the early morning hours to attend school. Most adults spend their days in places they do not even like but they seem to have no choice. Now that we have established that God created the earth and everything in it [Psalms 24:1], would He have created a world with no purpose and also create humans like us who would know it has no purpose? No.

Many people find their lives being all about paying bills and having good times on Friday nights. This is the majority of people. It seems to be a cycle of surviving each day, making sure they earn enough for tomorrow's food. When they grow old enough to get married they do so and procreate. But, only to perpetuate the same cycle. Few people find fulfilment in what they do. Where purpose is not known, there is bound to be abuse.

As established in the very first chapters of this book, God created man to be His vice-regent on earth. And He gave man the mandate to dominate, replenish and fill the earth. This is the general purpose of mankind on earth. As the human race, we have collectively achieved some great feats in as far as development is concerned. We have seen man conquering the sky and flying to cities in hours. We have seen the great pirates conquer the sea. Landscapes and rough terrains have been negotiated. Diseases have been cured. Recipes have been developed. The airwaves have been harnessed to transport voices and test to distant places. A lot is still to come. We have also fallen short in many regards. We have failed to maintain the world in a balance that promotes life. Global warming is a man-made problem. The world has seen slave trade, colonialism and now, neo-colonialism. We have seen great wars and great evil in places like Auschwitz. Multiplication has not been a problem at all. The means with which it is done makes it fairly easy.

All this, on a global scale, is a result of the cumulative efforts of individuals that have trodden the earth. There was one of us who discovered fire. There was another who discovered magnetic stone et cetera. Then some of us thought they were superior to the other races and decided to enslave others. Some of us loved power and money than people and decided to sell sex slaves. The list goes on and on. But the bottom line is that the world is in this state, good or bad, as a result of the works of individuals that have been on it.

Whether each man lived his purpose is another thing. But I guarantee you that some lived their purpose and brought good to the world. Others did not live their purpose but managed to do some good. Then others managed to do more bad than good. Some were fulfilled and some were not. Never settle for paying bills, eating good meals, enjoying vacations, driving a nice car, living in a nice house and sending your kids to the best schools. Much good in this world has been done by men and women who lived their purpose.

# Feedback Channels

I will gladly appreciate any comments, suggestions or any form of feedback on this book. Feel very free to contact me on these channels:

| | |
|---|---|
| Email | beansrobson@gmail.com |
| Phone/WhatsApp | 0027 71 564 4280 |
| Facebook | robson.beans |
| Twitter | @BeansRobson |
| | |
| Website | https://beansrobson.com |
| | |

www.ingramcontent.com/pod-product-compliance
Lightning Source LLC
Chambersburg PA
CBHW031140130726
47988CB00006B/2465